AF595579

A Good Family

A Good Family

Murder, Silence, and a Search for Meaning

Fredi Cooper and Jo Ann Caplan

Published by: MartinMidrash Press
511 E, Willow Grove Ave.
Wyndmoor Pa. 19038

First hard copy printing 2022
Title: A Good Family: Murder, Silence, And a search for meaning
Identifier: ISBN 979-8-9872212-0-4
Subjects: Family memoir, Forgiveness, Crime in Philadelphia Pa and New Jersey

"For Marty": The Last Word, by Gaeton Fonzi, *Philadelphia Magazine*, September 1972. Used by permission of *Philadelphia Magazine*.

Editorial: Anne Dubuisson
Text and cover design: Daniel Kohan, Sensical Design

"People were always so envious of our family because we were such a good family and everyone thought we were the perfect family." —Lucille Cohen Hess

Acknowledgements

Fredi

THIS BOOK PROJECT came about in anticipation of my retirement from an active rabbinic life. As I looked ahead, I knew that I wanted to come out of the dark and finally understand what had happened to my brother and to my family. Initially, I brought this idea to a group of rabbinic colleagues and formed a writing group with them. I want to thank those rabbis: Nancy Fuchs-Kreimer, Margot Stein, Linda Holtzman, Vivie Mayer and my colleague Susan Berman for joining me in this group. They were my first audience for some of this story. They encouraged me to continue writing. They helped to perfect the writing and they were my champions always reiterating that this was a story that needed to be told. Their belief in this book really was the fuel that kept me going.

Ultimately, I realized that my natural partner in this project was my sister, JoAnn. She and I have lived every moment of our lives together and she is my closest advocate and friend in addition to my sister. It was a long process filled with love and tears, to get all of this written. It is a reflection of our family and our devotion to each other that we were blessed to do this together.

My husband, Heshie, has championed every project I have undertaken in our lifetime together. He has been by my side always in writing this story and we have cried together often, over our sadness that we had not better understood Martin.

My daughters, Julie and Emily have been my inspiration for most of my life missions. They have both allowed me to grow and expand in watching the women that they have become. They have lived their lives in the shadow of this story and have held me close in my desire to understand it for myself and thus a bit better for them. Every word written has been read and lovingly approved by both of them. It is a blessing in life to have daughters who can contribute to every aspect of my life, as their mother.

We were extremely fortunate to have the expertise of Anne Dubuisson in editing this manuscript. Aside from the editing, Anne also believed in this project and has supported its ongoing revision. She has not allowed us to give up on what she deemed a worthy book.

I feel indebted to friends who always support all of my efforts in life and have understood the importance of this project especially, at this time in life. Thank you the myriad friends, for always encouraging and loving me in life, no matter what!

Jo Ann

I WOULD LIKE to express my appreciation to the Glenside library where we first began our memoir experience. The courses stimulated our interests and encouraged us to pursue our journey. The regular sharing and exchange of information and insights provided the reassurance that our story was worth telling.

Thanks also to family members who offered suggestions and critiques throughout the writing experience: my husband, Steve; my sons, Rick and Paul; and to many friends who have shared our lives: the challenges, the hardships and the high points. Our children's participation in our lives and the lives of their grandparents made the story valuable to retell. It is my hope that this book will remain an important and meaningful source of understanding and pride to our families and grandchildren.

Prologue

Martin and Jo Ann

Fredi

WHEN MY BROTHER Martin was murdered, I lived in a different city than the rest of the family. I came home only occasionally; more often my parents came to stay with me to escape their new reality. Once he was gone a deep and enduring silence fell over the family where anything connected to Martin was concerned. For me that silence meant that Martin had just disappeared. There was no finality. I never even attended his funeral. I felt "he was gone" from my life but it remained quite unreal. I often fantasized that I would be the one in the family to discover that he was really still alive in some remote place. In the recesses of my mind then I felt that if I were to find him somewhere, this time I could save him. I could finally rehabilitate him.

Away from all of the media coverage of his death and the apprehension of his murderers I lived in a state of total ignorance. Connected to this ignorance was also denial. I was able to live a "new life" in another city divorced from the scandal that enveloped the end of Martin's life.

I was absent from what was transpiring, but I always wanted to know what had happened and why it had happened to my brother.

I almost uncovered some information just months after he was gone. I was at my parent's home and found an envelope that contained clippings and magazine articles related to Martin's death. It was in my hand. I was all ready to delve into its contents, when the gentle hand of my mother caught me in this act and tore them away from me. I was ashamed of my action, and could not even face my mother once I was "found out."

The envelope continued to live in my imagination. I promised myself that one day I would get back to discovering its mysterious contents. I felt certain that Martin would have wanted me to.

The envelope remained elusive for many years, given the all-consuming demands of my young children and personal and professional development. Then there were the years of helping my parents to go on living with the family promise of deep silence. It was understood: The envelope could not be mentioned, much less opened.

Mother was still alive. I could not write the story. It would be too painful for her if she ever found out what I was up to. If I found my "own envelope" full of clippings about Martin, I might have had to talk with her about what I had found and what it meant to her. I knew that I could not do this in her lifetime.

And so, the envelope remained closed. It was always there in the recesses of my mind. I always knew that I would open it one day. Once I determined that I could even approach the possibility of creating my own envelope, I recognized that once I had one this would be what I wanted to write about in the years of my retirement.

The only other person I knew who had had a brother murdered by the mob was my own older sister, Jo Ann. Yet she and I had never adequately discussed his murder and the impact it had had on each of us, and on the families we had raised, almost side by side. She and I had bought into the family vow of complete silence and upheld that vow while our parents lived, even between us. Well after their deaths I wanted to finally break open that silence. I knew that I would need to appeal to my sister about this and possibly even invite her into my journey and my writing.

At first reluctant, Jo Ann agreed to join me, even though we had different goals in mind. We have been honest with each other about the difference in our goals for this project and the difference in our needs to revisit all of the details of Martin's life and death. I have wanted to know more of these as I was absent from the aftermath and thus missed much of the initial media coverage. In contrast, Jo Ann and her family were confronted daily by the onslaught of news coverage, so she felt no need to delve into the details again all these years later. Yet we both realized we needed to develop this story, and that there was an important family story to tell.

When I finally held the first clipping in my envelope in front of my eyes, my hands began to shake and a deep nausea enveloped me, just like the day when Martin was murdered. The emotions were as raw and as fresh as that day, August 7, 1972. Seeing my brother's body carried from the exploded car finally erased any lingering crazy doubts that he had really been murdered.

As sisters we know we must push past the sick feeling that this story has reawakened. We know that we are in a season of life where personal legacies have gained greater urgency. Time has beckoned to both of us and we now can no longer push it away. Our legacy is one of a particular family, one of whose members was brutally murdered. My sister and I can tell this story for all three of us. Martin's voice has called to us to do so, before it is too late and the silence endures.

Martin

JULY 2017

Dear Fredi,

It's been quite a long time since you have heard from me, it seems. I am contacting you from beyond. What does that mean "from beyond"? As you well know, I have been gone for forty-five years and I had hoped that by now someone would have been curious enough to find out what happened to me and why.

I am not sure that you are aware that forty five years ago I contacted an author, Gaeton Fonzi, when I felt desperate about the situation I had gotten myself into. I knew no way out. I was stuck in a world of gangsters, people who, as you know, we were not raised to understand. And competing with that was our parents telling me to "do the right thing and turn those gangsters in." Speaking to Fonzi I thought might allow my fate to be publicized and somehow save me from the forces that were pulling me under. I abandoned that project when my lawyer told me that it was not advisable. So I had hoped that after I was gone, someone would care enough to tell my story. I wanted it told because it was a cautionary tale that provided the background and the consequences to anyone else that might be tempted to try to "get rich quick" by tying their fate to the underworld. I learned too late that once you enter into that world there would be no easy way out.

So why am I writing to you, my little sister, so many years later? Up until the very end I was connected to you and we did share important parts of our lives together. Several times in the years when I had already been involved with a totally different life than our family life, I tried to tell you something about myself, but it was clear to me after my weak attempts that you were too naïve to understand the totality of me. So many years later, I wonder from this well-settled grave, if your life has developed in ways that you could now better understand me. I wonder if you still think of me and try to reconcile who "we" were with who I became? If you have come to such a place I want to issue an invitation to you, and maybe to Jo Ann as well, to investigate my story and write what I asked Fonzi to write so many years ago. It seems to me that if anyone would be able to speak to both sides of the picture, the story, it would be my siblings, the ones who shared those formative years with me so long ago. The two of you know my father and mother and you know all of the messages that we were sent. You two know the place that I inhabited as the first-born Jewish son. I am no longer able to recount my life legacy, but you can. I am asking you to do this for me. Perhaps it will be worthwhile for you as well.

I hope the forty-five years have treated you well. You were such an innocent when I knew you so many years ago. You seemed to embrace the conventional life and all that it offered. I hope that this embrace has served you well. I have so many fond memories of crazy times that we spent together. You were always open to me and game to come along on my adventures. I regret that I had to hold back so much of myself from all of you. I did this out of two kinds of fear. Fear of you knowing all of me and disapproving heartily, and fear for all of you too, as the people I was involved with were dangerous. Please know that there is so much about my life to regret, but also much of my life to remember fondly.

I hope that you will be able to accept my invitation. It would mean a great deal to me to realize that even after so many years, my family has come to know me and forgive me. I will await your answer.

With great fondness,
Martin

Jo Ann: A two-sided coin

RICHARD RUSSO SHARES, “The world is divided between kids who grew up wanting to be their parents and those who grow up wanting to be anything but. Neither group ever succeeds.”

Eleanor Roosevelt wrote that as we age, “We learn who we really are and then live with that decision.”

I am conflicted by the two-sided perspective that arises because Martin was a two-sided coin who embraced both good and evil. Generally his affect was unpredictable. When manic, he could generate excitement and enthusiasm for every one of his endeavors, from record hops to movie openings to the drapery business. The positive energy always rose to a climax that eventually ended badly. It is hard to remember an effort that ended successfully.

The act of writing the story will also be two-sided. Although we share many of the memories, mine are colored by a longer time frame that ended with an on-the-ground daily exposure to the disaster as portrayed by the press and the media. It was inescapable: on the daily news, TV and radio. That Fredi’s perception was removed by time and place has resulted in a strong curiosity to “learn the facts”, while my perception does not invite retrospection. As with a coin, when you flip it over, it looks different. One could choose to reflect only on the good side. What’s been lost following Martin’s death is we were never permitted or encouraged to remember either side.

The chore for the memoir writer is to compose a shape that gives faithful, reliable coherence to the many unequal things any life contains. It provokes an urge to reconcile the self-now with the self-back-then. Therefore, the memoir writer is never just a teller of other people's stories, but a character in those stories. Perception, in our case, is a two-sided coin. I believe my "up close and personal" reflects an on-the-ground daily exposure to the disaster as portrayed by the press and the media.

In our case, writing this memoir has allowed us, as sisters, to share feelings and misgivings we were never able to even contemplate before the death of our parents. In my case, this effort was a struggle to relive and recapture memories that had been buried in my personal space for over 45 years. Fredi had a genuine commitment to uncovering "what really happened" prior to his death, in court hearings and newspaper reporting. I never wanted to revisit these sites as they evoked so many painful memories. In the end, it was the degree of Fredi's determination that convinced me to collaborate.

Mary Pipher writes in *Women Rowing North*, "There are many lifetimes in a lifetime. Our work together is a testament to that reality." When I think about life and career changes each of us has made in the course of 70-plus years, I recognize the significance of our relationship as we matured. It is a relationship that has been nurtured like a fine wine: in times of trouble, sorrow, wavering health, emotional challenges and successes. Everything considered in retrospect accounts for the cherished place each of us has in our shared lives.

THE LAST WORD

For Marty

by Gaeton Fonzi

Getting in was easy. But getting out . . .

Several months ago, Paul Rubin and Marty Hess wrote to me for help. "There is no way we could describe the past years of our lives in this letter," they wrote. What they did describe was enough for me to contact them and begin what may eventually be one of the most bizarre and revealing stories I've ever done.

Paul and Marty turned out to be two young men who ran a small drapery business in Marlton, N.J. Several years ago, as bright, inquisitive kids, they had been moved by peer values into the drug culture of their times. Not the hard stuff, just pills, grass and hashish. From buying they went to dealing and from dealing they went into bigger dealing. Soon they were part of a very profitable operation, a thrice-weekly shuttle from the West Coast that supplied a good percentage of all the marijuana coming into the Philadelphia area.

They made a lot of money, an awful lot of money, and maybe it was the money that turned their heads and didn't let them see just how big they were getting and where they were heading. The problem was that they were getting too big and before they knew it they were swept into an expanding circle of contacts with associates from the major leagues, including corrupt police officials and men with connections to organized crime.

Soon the deals they became involved with got even bigger and more sinister, took on international aspects and involved very big men with legitimate fronts, including a prominent Philadelphia doctor and a friend of a top public official.

And then the bubble burst for Paul and Marty. A series of arrests put them on a merry-go-round of another kind of dealing—with law enforcement agencies. They avoided it as long as they could because they could afford to. They spent hundreds of thousands of dollars in lawyers' fees, bail bond costs and bribes. A family business was put into bankruptcy to raise even more money. But the pressure was put on them and kept on them until they began cooperating with the law.

And the law wanted more and more. When they resisted they were

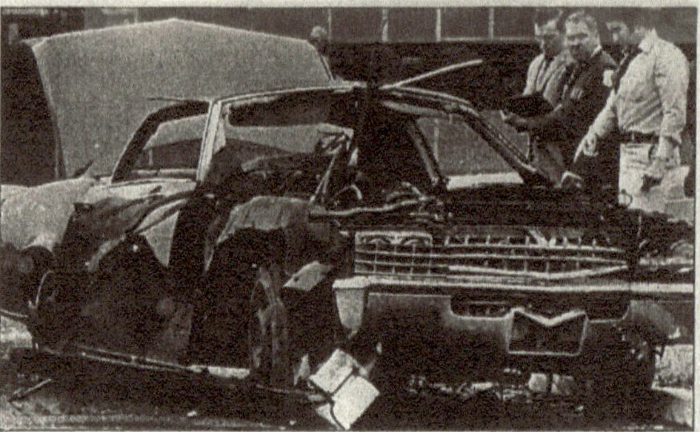

Phila. Daily News

hit with additional charges, either dug up from a corner of their past or newly and deliberately manufactured. They tried to resist—Marty even spent six months in jail—but the law used even the most despicable methods to keep the pressure on, including the manipulation of personal friendships. They were dealing with at least five federal and local law enforcement agencies and each wanted to suck them for its own glory. In fact, one was willing to provide them with a large amount of cash to finance a trip to Jamaica where they could buy and smuggle back a load of grass in order to set up additional arrests. A legal purist might insist that involved entrapment, but what the hell if the charges didn't hold up, the agency's arrest statistics would get a shot in the arm.

Obviously the law wasn't concerned with the morality of playing with the lives of informants, but from a practical viewpoint Paul and Marty were promised plenty of protection. And that's what they got: promises of protection and more pressure to turn in more people.

That's when they contacted me. They were desperate. They were on a merry-go-round they couldn't get off. As the law put more pressure on them so did their former associates, especially the big ones with connections. They were very much afraid and couldn't figure out what to do until they came up with the idea that maybe a magazine article or maybe even a book about their experience might get them the publicity and notoriety that would take the heat off them personally.

I remember, when I first met Paul and Marty, being struck by how unlikely a pair they seemed to be involved in the hard world of crime. Paul was tall and thin with a boyishly handsome face and long brown hair that flowed to his shoulders. Marty was shorter and heavier and had a fine crop of wild curly hair and dark gentle eyes. In fact, that's what especially attracted me to the story, that they were both gentle, intelligent young men who were sensitive enough to recognize and communicate the emotional impact of their desperate situation. We sat for hours that first evening we met over coffee in the kitchen of Paul's rustic home in Medford Lakes, myself and an associate, Paul and his wife Candy, Marty and a friend, planning the days of tape-recorded sessions that would lay the groundwork for the story. Although they were scared and hesitant initially, as they unfolded the details of their dealings they became more excited and eager as they recognized their lives had indeed become quite an adventure. They were like a couple of kids.

Not that they didn't know the seri-

(continued on page 146)

The Last Word

continued from page 220

ousness of their situation. I remember having dinner with them one night in the new Holiday Inn in Cherry Hill. They had gone ahead with the idea of getting together with me without consulting their lawyer and then began to have some doubts about it and thought maybe we should at least discuss the project with him. They said he was a good guy who, they believed, had always leveled with them. Let's see what he thinks, they said.

He didn't think the project was such a good idea. He was pretty strong in his feelings about it and we kicked it around for a couple of hours. Paul and Marty didn't say much but they listened carefully and it soon became obvious that the lawyer wasn't objecting to it on principally legal grounds. He kept trying to talk it down in terms of editorial interest and said that readers wouldn't care what happens to a couple of drug dealers.

As more time went by, Marty Hess knew he was going to get more pressure to turn more people in, and that would increase the pressure from the other side and the merry-go-round would roll even faster.

Marty was suddenly quiet but I could see the circles forming in his mind.

They were really confused when I left them that night. Paul said that maybe they were getting a little paranoid because so much pressure had been on them for so long. Marty was sullen and worried because the law was pressuring him to testify in a couple of big cases coming up, one against a police lieutenant and the other against a South Philly racketeer. Paul said that Marty, for the first time, was really getting concerned for his life.

Those kinds of fears are something you talk about, as we did that night, with a certain dash of fantasy. I've been involved in a few stories over the years where threats have come up, when the possibility of violence and death has been talked about, but always in a kind of remote way. You don't take them seriously. Bravery and courage have nothing to do with it because both of those words are meaningless, phony and arbitrary judgments of a man. Every man does what he can do and the only time he is not afraid is when he is able not to think about it.

As I left Marty Hess that night he was thinking about it and he was afraid and I could see the concern in his gentle face. I remember standing in the parking lot after we left the restaurant, he, Paul and I, not speaking, just standing there confused and frustrated, not knowing whom to trust or what to do or how to stop the merry-go-round. But because their lawyer was so opposed to our continuing the story, we decided to put things aside for a while and see what happened. So we stood there after reaching that inconclusion and the frustration of it all seemed the greatest in Marty. As more time went by he knew he was going to get more pressure to put more people in and that would increase the pressure from the other side and the merry-go-round would roll faster. After our long silence, Marty just shook his head and when he looked up at me I saw in his soft dark eyes the deepest despair I've ever seen in any man's eyes. "O.K.," he said simply, without resolution or finality, shook my hand and turned and walked away.

Then late one morning last month, Paul called me. He told me that Marty had just been blown up in his car. It had happened outside of Marty's apartment in Cherry Hill and Paul had rushed right over but Marty was dead when he got there, lying in the back seat. Paul said he called me right away because he knew I would want to know and to tell me that he still wanted to go ahead with what we started. Not right now, he said, because he would probably be put into protective custody and then go away for a while, move to another place and change his name. But he said that someday he would get back to me and we would do it. He really wanted to do it now, he said. And so do I, I told him. ■■

PART I

An American Story

Our mother

Jo Ann

LAURA SILLERMAN RELATES *that "Families exist to witness each other's disappointments." In fact, we were more witness than participant, and that is what is most disturbing in retrospect. Although Martin's issues were always front and center in our household, our interaction was to be on the sidelines watching... incapable of providing any support... our insights were of little consequence and offered no solutions.*

In the neighborhood, we all followed Martin's lead. We looked for buried treasure in that forbidden lot where I broke my tooth. I paid for my transgression with many hours at the dentist. He was never forgiven for leading me down that path. We always went to the movies together, at the Ogontz, in West Oak Lane, Philadelphia, two miles from out home.... But, he convinced us that for the same $.25, we could watch the film: Tea for Two" over. We loved that movie. We went to a matinee on a Sunday and stayed till 8:00 p.m. Oh boy, was there hell to pay when we returned. No more movies! No dinner! Spanking... right to bed. What did we know about parental fears?! What we learned was more about punishment for youthful curiosity than grown-up worry. We certainly had that fear ingrained in our daily existence. One never wanted to anger our father... even for minor things like putting the heat on or leaving the top off the toothpaste. His rage was terrifying to me but did not frighten our brother in the same way. In fact, it became the impetus for trying risky behaviors throughout his life. In Martin's baby book, under "First Words" is written: August 1942, "Da-Da, Bad Boy."

Contemplating family dynamics acknowledges that "life can only be understood backward." Who was Martin Alan Hess? In the mind of his mother, he was her fantastical hope and dream. She was so moved by Sinclair Lewis's Arrowsmith that she named her first born Martin, after the lead character. Her personal and familial background interest in medicine provoked this hope. The novel portrays a character so intrigued with medicine that he begins to study Gray's Anatomy at age 14. This mirrored mother's predisposition to medicine. Ironically in the novel, the lead character's first marriage ends in divorce as the first wife is focused only on money and position rather than the search for truth. Mother's marriage was confounded by similar dilemmas.

Mary Gordon writes in her memoir, The Shadow Man Knowing My Father, that her writing allows her to "make peace with what he did as a parent." I believe my writing is also an attempt to arrive at some intangible peace derived from the efforts we shared. Like Mary Gordon, my father arrived in America in the great wave of immigration at the end of the 19th and beginning of the 20th century. Unlike Gordon's father, my father arrived as an orphan at a time when it seemed endlessly possible for young men to make and remake themselves. My father fully subscribed to the "golden opportunity" in the way he carried himself and behaved until he married at age 33, he was a typical "lady's man" enamored with the morays of the American dream.

Whether he ever realized it in his life, my father's affect had the greatest impact on the shape of his son's life. Martin pursued an American dream of wealth obtained by any means. My father used to tell us as a young man he was "a big shot." My brother's demise was, in part, shaped by that expectation. In a different time and century, he pursued the American dream of wealth and fame and perished in his efforts.

Opposites attract, so they say

HE WAS THIRTY two... dashing... outgoing... funny... and seemingly worldly.

She was just nineteen... almost ready to graduate, first in her class, from Albert Einstein Nursing school. She was quiet, studious, very intelligent and pretty.

They met on a weekend stay at a kosher farm in New Jersey. It was a place where young Jewish people went to find a partner.

These were our parents, Lucille Cohen and Samuel Hess. They succeeded in their pursuit.

Their backgrounds were as disparate as those cursory descriptors above.

My father was from Austria or Poland or the Ukraine... the place of birth often changing depending on when the story was told and who told it. They were a Hasidic family of seven children born in a Shtetl. The family story was that my father's father was a bootlegger and his "refinery" was in their home in this small village. My father attended a Cheder (a religious school) in which the boys were taught by the village rabbi. He told stories of sitting by the rabbi's side and learning all of our religious texts. My father's parents died in a very short period of time leaving four of the children alone in the village as orphans. Their oldest brother, Joseph/Wolfe was killed, it was said, serving the army in the war. (We recently learned he may actually have been murdered as a result of his involvement with crime. Hmmm!... a family dynamic.) My father had little to say about what it meant to be an orphan.

The Hess sisters and our father arrived in the United States in 1921. Their passage was financed by Lou Hamerling, a distant cousin who had made a fortune in the U.S.; and who was able to supply $2,000.00 to ensure their journey. Although dad always told the story that he was 11 years old upon arrival; he was, in fact either 16 or 17. It was significant that they lied about his age because at 17, he was eligible to serve in the army during World War I. If they had waited, his fate would have been conscription; and, having already lost parents and an older brother the family longed for safe passage.

The story dad always told about how he was the "darling" little boy on the ship was in fact an embellishment. He was small, wiry and charming. These traits enabled him access to passengers who needed favors which he was happy and adept at providing He had a magnanimous ability to relate to people, to schmooze; a trait that provided him with entry to a lifetime career.

The siblings came to the states and moved in initially with their oldest sister Anne in Philadelphia. My father spent a very short period of time in school once he was in America. School held little allure for Samuel, he was much happier finding jobs to do and he was very adept as both a salesman and as a schmoozer. Very quickly he was out on the street, doing business, selling linens and making connections with merchants. He spoke no English but learned quickly how to navigate the American landscape. He never graduated from high school but he was determined to capture the "American Dream." For him that dream was to demonstrate his success as an American by proving to be a "ladies" man with many conquests and getting employment that allowed him to purchase a car, something few were able to do at the time.

My mother, Lucille, was born in Philadelphia to a mother who was also born in Philadelphia and a father who had come to the states as a little boy. So my mother's family was already quite assimilated to American family values and had a very different approach to life. My grandfather Philip was an excellent student who had been accepted to a medical school program at Jefferson Hospital. When his family could not afford for him to pursue this pathway he went on to study Pharmacology and became a licensed pharmacist, a job he held his entire life. Rose came from a traditionally religious family: but willfully abandoned its tenets in her marriage. Her intention and drive in raising her family was to assimilate to the "American" way: i.e., to adhere to WASP societal norms, which had no place for Jewish religious practice. Traditional American families went to church on Sundays and celebrated American holidays like Halloween, Thanksgiving and Christmas. It was expected that the children in the family would marry well and live a life that reflected success. Our grandmother Rose, always dressed like she was a wealthy woman, fashioning her appearance after those wealthy WASP women she encountered in fashion magazines. She was quite snobbish about this and would only shop in certain department stores in Center City Philadelphia; Wanamaker's and Bonwit Teller.

Lucille was a strong student from day one. She excelled at a very competitive Philadelphia high school and graduated at age 16, having skipped several grades. She applied to the University of Pennsylvania and was accepted, but like her father was not able to find the funds to attend. She pursued her second choice, the nursing program at Albert Einstein Hospital. This appealed to her as it allowed her to live on campus for three years, independent of her family. She had to lie on her application about her age as she was technically too young to attend the program. Her age would never be discovered as she was always the most mature and serious student, graduating first in her class.. She was able to pass her Nursing boards with ease. Her studies always came first and she had little interest in dating.

So from two different universes Samuel and Lucille met on that farm in New Jersey. He was smitten with her beauty, she was taken with this "older man," so experienced at life and flashy with self-confidence. They quickly became a couple.

My father's family was delighted by this development. My mother was everything and more than they could have dreamt of for my father.

My mother's family, Rose in particular, was devastated. Her daughter's suitor was a "greenhorn" and so much less than what she dreamed of for her daughter: an immigrant, without even a high school diploma!, uneducated, too outgoing, very(!) Jewish, and a salesman! Her daughter was worthy of so much more in her eyes.

And so, the beginning was not smooth. My father's family, always warm and enveloping to the couple. My mother's family, always distant and aloof. My father and his mother-in-law never made peace. My mother remained close to her parents and they were central to our childhood, joining us for dinner every Sunday. But the tension was always present. My grandmother often absented herself from the table if she found my father objectionable. If dinner was at her house, she would just keep herself distant from him by being busy in the kitchen. However, when dinner was at our house, she literally would sit in the kitchen with our maid, Ocie Mason, to avoid my father and his all- knowing manner. My father would complain about going where he wasn't respected or welcome. Once we arrived, he would complain about how hot they kept the apartment.

Opposites attract.

Our father: Outgoing, fiery, street smart, religious, lovable, extravagant, sowed his wild oats, family oriented, moody, schmoozy, uneducated, opinionated, authoritarian, funny.

Our mother: Smart, educated, ambitious, striving, loving, quiet, appealing, calm, a thinker, elegant, classy, extravagant, children come first, serious.

Our parents were married in August of 1939; on the precipice of US involvement in World War II. Our father, Samuel had just turned thirty-four.

As the marriage commenced, so did our father's domination. His dominion included insistence on the observation of Jewish customs that Lucille's parents had worked to put behind them. Samuel insisted on teaching his new wife how to create a "Jewish Home."

From the outset of this marriage, there was never any question about who was in charge or who ruled the roost. My father was much older than my mother: he had overcome life hardships, established a career for himself with many accoutrements of success. He sported Stetson hats and always smoked El Producto cigars. These were elements of a "successful salesman's wardrobe" and attitude. My mother felt subservient to him from the get- go and, because of the age disparity, his rules were the laws of our household.

When Martin was born, on our parents' 2nd anniversary, the atmosphere or environment changed. My father's place of importance was challenged by his first child. My mother's role was enhanced by it. Martin became central to her existence and would remain her number one concern until his dying day. His arrival threatened my father's position of dominance at the same time as it demanded he expand his repertoire to include fathering; a role he believed had to include a stern demeanor and acts of punishment when his rules were challenged. One did not dare to challenge his authority or his beliefs. Any attempt to make a point or to take a position contrary to his, was met with nasty and recriminating response.

One cannot be certain, in retrospect, what Dad's expectations for his son would be. One can only reflect on the pride and the challenges that go hand-in-hand with raising a family. Of course there were financial risks and rewards. Owning their first home came with expectations that they would "keep up with the neighbors." They were always ultra-aware of the financial successes and acquisitions of those to either side of them.. At the same time, they were always apprehensive about how they fit in and how they could acquire all of the elements of success. Growing up close to my brother, he made me aware of what we didn't have that others did on a constant basis.

Martin's desire to acquire those signs of success were inculcated very early in our lives. Our neighbors had a piano and a trumpet and music lessons and the first television set to arrive on the scene. We spent lots of time camped out in their house because they had what we could not afford. After all, their father was a professional... a dentist, while ours was a "schlepper" of dry goods from customer to customer.

Mother would apply economic pressure to ensure we measured up to friends and neighbors whose status she regarded as better than ours. This behavior was likely part of her upbringing as Grandmother Rose always took care to never mingle with anyone beneath her perceived status.

As my brother grew, he could only be regarded as a handsome little boy whose resemblance to his mother was keen. My arrival 2½ years later provided my father with offspring who more closely resembled him and who, therefore, had special approval from him.

In the early stages of family life there was no indication of a child who had a problem. However, upon entry to a public school for gifted students, Martin began to evidence behaviors that would lead to a lifetime realization that "he wasn't living up to his potential." Around the middle of first grade Martin developed rheumatic fever which turned him into a bed-ridden invalid for four months. He became his mother's project. As a nurse, she was ultra-sensitive to his every need, bringing favored foods to his bedside, entertaining him with games, puzzles, stories and art projects. In the late 1940's little was understood about this disease which today would be treated with medication and little or no bed rest. In those days absolute bed rest was mandated. I can vividly recall my father's displeasure with the time and attention proffered to Martin. I can remember sitting on the steps outside of his room entertaining myself with young reader books while my mother attended to his needs.

This illness established a dynamic dysfunction to my parents' relationship and created dissension between my father and brother that lasted a lifetime. At the same time, Martin was learning the skill of playing one parent against the other. He began to learn exactly how to get to his mother's heart while simultaneously angering his father's temperament. As a sibling, I would witness this tension played and replayed throughout his life.

Mother recognized early on that Martin was not the ordinary child who worked to gain parental approval by doing well in school or even by behaving appropriately. In the current school environment he would be classified as learning disabled, having enough natural intelligence to be successful in learning but not having the necessary individual help to allow him to succeed in school. When frustrated by his lack of understanding, he would act in ways classified as "behavior problems." These were actually the result of his frustration with not succeeding.

In fact, I asked several pointed questions about the way our parents disciplined us... their children. My mother shared she was upset by my father's need to slap/beat Martin for behaviors at age 4 when they were away at the shore with another family. That family, who were friends at the outset, had a very different... more tolerant way of disciplining. This was not something my father could abide by. In his life, he was used to a "zest in pisque" (slap in the face) when he stepped out of line. He related that his mother tried to shield him (under her skirt) from his father's anger. He was the youngest child in the family. That method did not always work.

The punishing (hitting) aspect of discipline was learned behavior for my father and aberrant for my mother. In every instance, she was unable to change his aggressive responses to any of Martin's shenanigans. Rather, he would become infuriated and lash out at him for trivial as well as major instances of mischief. He wasn't going to "let him get away with anything."

This became the challenge to Martin's affect early on. It was almost routine for Martin to do things that he knew would initiate and anger dad. How could Dad be expected to love and respect this child who was always promoting trouble?!

In truth, this might have been the only way to get his father's interest.

PART II

A Typical Jewish Family

Our family

Jo Ann

"We look at the world once, in childhood. The rest is memory." —Louise Glück

UPON REFLECTION, I *can recall so many instances when my brother was the "leader of the band"; the creative thinker who could produce both wonder and magic at times. In the early years after Fredi was born, he was my hero who constantly introduced me to a world where anything and everything was exciting and could happen any time, any day. I would follow him on adventures though the neighborhood. There was the vacant lot at 18th and Stenton that people used as a waste site: discarding a variety of unwanted stuff. He believed there was treasure buried there and we combed through the detritus we were "forbidden" to explore. That's how I fell and broke my front tooth which resulted in unnecessary pain and expense for the family. It was "my fault" because I was dumb enough to follow my brother.*

The summer Grandpop died was the summer Martin and I were planning to "run away" in his new Ford Falcon. There had been many loud and punishing arguments about the way each of us was "wasting" time and were not living up to parental expectations. At the precipice of our plans, Pop-Pop became increasingly sick and I would leave my volunteer post at Einstein Hospital in the afternoon and go to University of Pennsylvania Hospital to be with him. I was the only one there the afternoon he died. That chapter ended our escape plans.

Whether he was planning a dance, a rock and roll benefit or opening a new stall at a farmer's market, Martin's mind was always being creative. He started collecting records at the outset of "Bandstand": Frankie Lymon, "Why Do Fools Fall in Love" as an example and played them in the living room on Williams Avenue after school. Mother pushed both of us to go to be "more social" and meet people. Martin saw it as an entrepreneurial opportunity... as he did at every turn in his life.

As we entered our teenage years, Mother insisted we learn to mingle with Jewish kids beyond the neighborhood. Martin learned about USY (United Synagogue Youth) from the dances he produced. He dragged me along and eventually we both joined the organization. Because of his entrepreneurial skills, he was elected our chapter president and the chapter became the most successful one in Philadelphia.

As a result of his leadership, we both traveled to local and national conventions, in Buffalo and Chicago. We met some terrific young people locally from Wynnefield and Norristown... and nationally from all over the U.S. Some USY members became our friends at Camp Sholom and throughout the year at USY events.

Martin's nature to characterize some of these friends was comedic, but also right on target. One girl, Marlene L., was very well-endowed and always wore a Muhlenberg sweatshirt. As a result of his exposure to her "Muhlenbergs" whenever he encountered any well-endowed female, his first description was always referenced to her Muhlenbergs. So many of the youth we met through USY went on to become successful adults and are today, still influential participants in the philanthropic Jewish community.

Martin could analyze situations and people very well and turn his analysis into a personal gain. He was never interested in friendships... rather what any relationship could bring him in fame or fortune. This was his undoing: in the end, the people he believed would advance his success in whatever illegal endeavor were actually never in his corner... always intent on getting rid of this cocksure individual.

It was his instinct to seek out the "forbidden, dangerous and illegal" because he believed he was always going to succeed when testing the limits. His life experiences bore that out in so many peculiar, distinct ways. He would be keenly interested when a new business like the Fruit Basket on Wadsworth Avenue opened. Whereas most people would just look at a new store and purchase items, he would study the "what, when, where, and how" of its evolution. He never needed textbook instruction when he could observe and ingest information and turn it into something creative and often successful.

Fredi: Cars, clothes

WE ARE ALL deep in preparation for Martin's Bar Mitzvah. It is the first big celebration of a milestone life cycle event in our immediate family. There is much emphasis on what we will all wear.

I had two new outfits. For Friday night Shabbat service I had the outfit most in vogue at that time, a pink felt "poodle skirt," and a matching shirt. My sister wore this same outfit, so we were dressed a bit like twins. For the dinner dance, I wore a red and white taffeta gingham dress that had velvet black ribbons on the skirt. I wore black velvet Mary Janes. My mother wore a pink satin dress for the dinner dance, it was adorned with teardrop shaped crystals. Mother's dress wound up being a centerpiece for the Bar Mitzvah.

The week before Martin's Bar Mitzvah, his one friend, Alan Elfman, had his Bar Mitzvah at our synagogue. The Elfmans were well- to- do and my brother wanted his Bar Mitzvah to be as special as Alan's was. Ironically, the stage at Alan's Bar Mitzvah was adorned from one end to the other with pink satin, with crystal drops making it sparkle. When Martin saw that on the stage... he immediately connected it to my mother's dinner dance dress and this had him ready to "make a deal" with the florist. On his own, he found out who had decorated the room that way and spoke to them and arranged somehow that the pink satin would remain in place until after his Bar Mitzvah was over the following Sunday. I have no idea what the deal was. Martin knew that the family could not afford another cent to be spent on the Bar Mitzvah dinner dance so he exchanged "something" for the pink satin. I can attest that the room looked much more impressive because of it.

We rode to the synagogue in our new 1954 Buick, crème de menthe green on the bottom with a darker green roof.

In all of the pictures for this occasion we look like the quintessential perfect Jewish family of the fifties. In particular, Martin looked his conservative best.

When Martin was sixteen, as soon as he could drive, he bought himself a used Chevy convertible, light blue with a beige canvas top. He bought the car for under one hundred dollars, which says a lot about its condition. I have a distinct memory that the top of the car was ripped, but he repaired it with masking tape.

When the Chevy died shortly after its purchase, my grandmother Rose, who loved Martin and wanted to please him gave him the money to purchase a new Ford Falcon. This car was pitch black inside and out... and really did not represent the image Martin wanted to put forth, but it was sturdy and reliable. So for a short while, his Falcon was like his Charcoal grey suit, muted and conservative... too much like the family's black Pontiac sedan.

As his choice of car continued to evolve to reflect how he saw himself, so ultimately did his clothes. Martin's clothes became flashier with each year. His suits; shiny and silky and loud. When it was in to wear bell bottoms... his pant legs were the widest... and his shirts the loudest. He liked to wear jewelry as well. A star sapphire ring... a diamond pinky ring... a flashy gold watch... all gifts to him from my mother always wanting to keep him happy even when she did not approve of this style. Not long after his Bar Mitzvah, Martin used his own money to purchase the forbidden "black leather jacket"... that the "bad boys" wore. When my parents discovered the jacket there was a scene... and Martin was told never to wear it again. He hid the jacket away and wore it only when my parents could not see him in it. But I did! When my parents went out on Sunday nights and the three of us were home the jacket would come out. Martin would let us know that he had "plans" that we were never to mention to our parents and that he was going "out." In order to fit in with whomever he was meeting the black leather jacket, was necessary. Jo Ann and I kept our part of the bargain and never let on that the jacket still existed and was in use.

And the car... the last car was a Cadillac El Dorado Convertible. It was gold and had leather seats. He drove it fast with the top down. It matched perfectly with his image... and it looked ridiculous parked in front of my parent's house or my sister's house...where the cars were mundane and commonplace.

Go ahead then, hit her back

I RUN INTO the kitchen on 18th street where my mother is ensconced in cooking in her sunny yellow kitchen... I grab her around the legs crying uncontrollably...

"Mommy, Jo Ann hit me again,. please get her to stop!" and my mother marched out of the kitchen telling me to wait right there and she brought Jo Ann to the kitchen and told me...you need to learn to hit her back... so go ahead and do it..

I raised my hand limply... and after a brief minute I said to my mother no... I cannot do it... I don't want to do it... I won't do it...

And mother warned me that if I had so little ability to fight back this would keep happening. Already at about four years of age I knew that hitting back was not for me and that I wanted no part of it. There were many other activities my family took part in and traits they exhibited that I sought to avoid. They included:

- Yelling at another in the family for a stupid reason
- Determining that only one way was the right way
- Labeling people for who they seemed to be in the family: "the bad one," "the smart one," "the weak one," "the sweet one"
- Willingness to break the rules and hide it from our parents
- Belittling someone who disagreed with you
- Being opinionated and sure you were right
- Bossing the other around or bullying behavior

- Causing my mother unhappiness
- Unreasonable outbursts of temper that seemed to come from nowhere

I was somewhat alone in the spot that I found myself in in this constellation, and for the most part this was 100 percent fine with me. As the youngest I found myself occupying a quiet observational corner. In this position I often asked myself: "What's wrong with what just transpired and how could that have gone in a better way?"(the budding family therapist at work.)

I would take my observations to my mother, the only one who would listen to me or I could trust to say what I needed to say. She always confirmed that I was right, but also shared that she felt as powerless as I did.

I was her daughter one hundred percent. I looked like her. I thought like her, I liked the same things as she did, but like me, she felt powerless amongst the strong currents that ran from my brother, my sister and my father.

She and I...we just treaded water... and watched...

In my mind and heart I was sure that if only they would listen to me I could make something better happen... but that's just where it stayed... mind and heart...

"Just hit her back!"...

I could not do it... I would not do it...

Those three seemed too strong for me to tangle with!

They would not listen to me

SO WHY WOULD I think that anyone would ever listen to me in my family?

In spite of all of that I tried. Even when I was very young, I tried.

I would say to my parents: Martin has a problem and surely there must be someone who can help him?"

I would say to my parents: "Our family has a problem and surely there must be someone who can help us?

I would say to my parents: "Martin is sweet and kind... so why do you always think he is bad?"

I would say to my parents: "You told me you would do something about Martin's problem and our problem and now you say everything is all okay. How did you decide that it was now all okay?"

I would say all of these things to them and in general my words were dismissed.

Their response was that I was over-reacting and that everything was under control. I knew even as a young child that these offerings were platitudes or just wishful thinking. I would persist in offering my opinion but at a certain point I always gave up. I accepted the role that I was cast in... and I admitted to myself that they would never listen to me.

This is who he was to me

MANY TIMES MARTIN was the one in charge of Jo Ann and me.

I find him in the kitchen: "So Martin what are you up to?"

He answers that he is baking me a cake and that I should wait in the living room until he is finished with the baking and he will serve it to me! I am intrigued... Hey Martin, what recipe are you using?

"I don't need a recipe I am making it up as I go along."... he answers

And so, I sit and wait... and then hear him laughing uncontrollably and shouting:

"You won't believe this... I must have put too much of something into the mix. The cake is exploding all over the oven... come fast... you have to see this!"

And what I saw was an oven, filled with cakes everywhere... bulging out of the pans... growing on the floor and shelves of the oven... he had put way too much baking powder in the mix... after all... no recipe... and the oven had become like a forest of cakes of all sizes!

It was a fantastic sight... but not a pretty one to have to clean up before our parents got home... and as we scooped up cakes of all sizes from the oven... we tasted a few... and they were vile!

Martin wasn't upset by the mess or by the outcome... not one bit! He was delighted that he had filled the oven with such fun!

Easter chicks

ONE DAY MARTIN walked into the house with three little "Easter chicks" that could be purchased right before the holiday. One was yellow, one dyed pink and one dyed blue. He was excited that he had gotten us "pets." Jo Ann and I did not know what to make of it... as we were not allowed to have a pet at that particular point and we did not know how to care for chicks! But we were all happy as we now felt that we could have a little piece of Easter right there in our house... as the Easter basket was off limits... as it was most likely Passover then, as well.

When we asked Martin how we would keep the chicks our secret, he said his plan was to keep them in a box and hide the box under the sofa in the living room. He felt certain that if they were kept there our parents would never catch on!

It did not take even an hour after my parents arrived home for the chicks to begin making noise... and for the discovery to be made. The chicks had to go of course... but the point is... he could always get Jo Ann and I to go along with him and suspend our reason in these schemes.

Even a hospital visit could be an adventure!

ONE YEAR, BOTH of my grandparents were in the hospital. My grandfather had an infection after surgery for his gallbladder and my grandmother had had a mild heart attack. We spent every weekend visiting them there and bringing them some Pesach food so that they did not miss the holiday entirely.

I fondly remember that on Sundays my brother and I would walk around the corner from the hospital to the Atwater Kent Museum, a maritime museum, not particularly riveting for children. However, as we walked he would come up with a different lens to view the exhibit through each time... or a made up maritime adventure for us to imagine as we walked through the exhibits. Martin would say: "This time we are going to pretend that we are the passengers on the ship and hope that there isn't a storm to contend with!" or "This instrument indicates that there is trouble ahead, I don't know if this ship can withstand this problem! What should we do now?"

What was best about the visits was the gift shop. He would always find something there to treat me to... "Look Fredi, he would say quite excitedly, that tablet has ships on the paper you really must have it!" Once those words came from his lips, I really did want that tablet!. The next week he might notice that there was a wooden figure of a ship captain. "I know your Ginny dolls would like to get to know the captain." The captain became Ginny's new friend as soon as we returned home that night.

When we walked back to the hospital I felt that visiting the grandparents was not so bad after all. I got time alone with Martin, an adventure and a souvenir too!

And the boardwalk!

MY FATHER'S SISTERS Lil and Gert lived in Atlantic City and many holidays included a visit to their apartment... all of the cousins... a walk on the Boardwalk and dinner at my aunts.

Easter Sunday was often also Pesach... and so the walk on the boardwalk was less fun because of the treats that were not permitted for us... the ice cream, the fudge, the hot dogs. Pesach is the holiday when the Jewish people mark the Exodus from Egypt. In the hurry to escape Egypt the bread prepared for the trip could not properly rise and so this was the beginning of the custom of eating matzah during the eight days of Pesach. With each generation there were more and more food restrictions that were added to assure that no bread product was ingested.

Martin always had a way of convincing the entire group of cousins that what we thought was not allowed for Pesach... actually was. We would therefore indulge in something that we should not indulge in and then he would report us for "breaking Pesach" as soon as we returned to the parents!

What he was a master of was playing the Boardwalk games. He was always able to earn enough tickets to redeem a gift for me or for my mother. For me it would be a new stuffed animal. One year he won a "deep fat fryer" for my mother, and it became a custom to make French fries in it... especially on Pesach!

Shabbat observed

MOTHER WORKED FULL time at the family business and so the preparation for Shabbat at this point rested on Ocie Mason, our maid. In the afternoon she would walk down Wadsworth Ave and purchase Challah and cake for the dinner and then spent the rest of her day in preparation for the meal.

Typical for this dinner was a roasted capon with a stuffing of little noodles and onion, a green vegetable and roasted potatoes. There might also be chicken soup as an appetizer. When I would walk into our house after school on those Fridays it smelled like Shabbat.

The table was set for three, Martin, Jo Ann and I and sometimes four if Mother was able to join us by dinnertime. Daddy was never at the table. He was always at the store on Shabbat eve, and some weeks mother also was there late and only made it home in time to take the three kids to Shabbat evening service at our synagogue, Congregation Emanu-El.

On those weeks when it was just the three of us Martin ruled the roost dictating whether we would luxuriate and enjoy our carefully prepared dinner or whether he would turn it into a contest of just how fast we could wolf it down. Jo Ann could be challenging for Martin in these contests as she had the habit of eating slowly... one food at a time and never mixing any of the vegetables with the chicken. I was much more compliant as I was always willing to "play" whatever game he came up with. So when it was just the three of us Shabbat dinner was finished in less than eight minutes... soup to cake. Then we awaited Mother to come home and pick us up to take us to synagogue, where we were left off to await her return once the store was closed for the night. If mother made it home for dinner there were no shenanigans. Dinner was to be savored and we were all to appreciate that we had mother at the table with us. We never let her know that if she was not present... dinner was a speed marathon.

The time in the synagogue was also influenced by whether mother was there with us. When we were dropped off we rarely made it into the sanctuary for the service. On those nights the synagogue became an amusement park funhouse. Martin knew all of the hidden passageways and secrets in that building. We followed him everywhere and he had stories to spin about why these secret places existed in our house of worship. This passageway is necessary in case the rabbi and the cantor need to escape if a ghost enters the building and wants to capture them! This is the place where that most unpopular Hebrew teacher actually lives! His interpretations were fantastical and not based on reality, but we loved to have him take us to the crazy places that he had invented. It was far!!! Better than sitting in the same service every week. Mother and Daddy would arrive around 9:00 PM so we had to be filing out of the sanctuary with all of the worshippers at that time so it would appear that when we were dropped off we went to the service. Once Mother and Daddy arrived it was off to the Oneg Shabbat, my second favorite part of Friday night Shabbat. There was a spread of a variety of cakes, my favorite one being the lemon roll and hot tea served in china cups. We were allowed to have as much as we wanted and I feel quite certain that I regularly had several pieces of that lemon roll.

Once we piled into the car to head home we knew that Daddy would come up with new "Shabbat restrictions" every week. We were told that we could not write, color, cut paper or wash our hair. If asked why we could not do these things, there was never an explanation. Other related activities for some reason seemed acceptable. We could listen to the radio, play records or watch TV. We could cook. It was best not to question Daddy as it might cause him to lose his temper... really fouling up the "Shabbat peace" at home. He often told us he wished he did not have to go to the store on Friday night or Saturday... being that it was Shabbat... but that was what was needed "when you are a retail merchant." This was just one more thing that made being the "retail merchant" such a hated way to make a buck. From the vantage point of the three Hess children, particularly Martin, there was nothing good about 6914 Torresdale Ave. It was a source of constant problems and a place that kept both of my parents from doing anything that they might have found satisfying in their lives.

Daddy wanted us to "keep Shabbat" for him in some way... since he could not. So this "keeping" involved several mixed up experiences... a Shabbat dinner that was generally "kids only," the kids supposedly "attending the service"... finally the family together at the Oneg Shabbat, and then home to "Shabbat restrictions" that made no sense whatsoever. And we did this religiously until we moved to our next home when I was ten years old.

What I held tightly to was that Shabbat dinner. When I began to make that dinner for my own family, I recreated the meal that Ocie had made for us. My children and my husband learned to identify and appreciate that its aroma spelled "Shabbat" in our home. If Martin were still alive he would find out that I now arrive in the sanctuary on time for Shabbat service and I pray... sometimes I am even the one who leads the service.

The Sukkah contest

I CAME HOME from Sunday school quite excited as my teacher invited all of us to make our own little sukkah and bring it in the next Sunday before Sukkot as an entry into a contest. The winning sukkahs would be displayed in the Synagogue hallway and the winner would receive a lovely piece of Judaica. I wanted to win the contest! It was just my type of project.

So I set about making that little sukkah right away. I got the shoe box from my closet and began by coloring in the walls. I made a little table out of the cardboard from the box top. I made some slates out of the box top for the roof. I remembered all of the things my teacher said were necessary to make the sukkah "kosher."

I excitedly brought my project to the Sunday night dinner table to show the family. My mother was encouraging about what I had accomplished. My father said it "looked kosher" to him. Jo Ann said this was something that she would never want to take part in, it seemed too stupid to her.

And then Martin piped up.

"You will never win the sukkah contest with that pathetic little sukkah. It will look just like everybody else's.. After dinner you and I will reconceive the sukkah so that yours will stand out! I would be embarrassed to have you take that one to Sunday school next week."

I felt a bit crushed by his comment... but also realized that maybe he was correct and so I let him know that I was game to let him help me to make my sukkah better.

No... Martin replied... we are not going to make that one better we will start all over.

And so we did, beginning that night.

Martin did not want the walls to be just the sides of a shoe box. He cut those sides out and then covered them with attractive wrapping paper before replacing them. Martin explained that the sukkah needed to be "outside" and so we fashioned a yard for it to stand in.

The next day, after he was finished with school, he went to Wadsworth Ave and bought materials. A sheet of pretend grass and popsicle sticks to build a fence in the yard. Cranberries for us to string across the roof. Martin used his own money. He always had money because even then... when he was just past his Bar Mitzvah, he worked at my parent's store and at the Drycleaner on Wadsworth Ave.

That night we stood the walls that we had completed the night before onto the grass yard and fashioned the fence around the yard. We made the roof and figured out how to string multiple strands of cranberries. The roof was perfect for a sukkah, one that provided shade while also letting some of the starlight in at night.

We made a new and more attractive table and several chairs and placed them in the sukkah. We used pictures from my mother's magazines to hang on the walls.

Martin wanted the table to be "set." So we made a tablecloth out of napkins. He suggested that there should be a challah on the table. So we used my new "Silly Putty" to make one and placed it on the table alongside a Silly Putty wine cup. The last thing on the table was a Silly Putty cornucopia, with beads in it to look like fruit and vegetables.

We placed one small branch on the table to look like a Lulav and a yellow bead for the Etrog.

Now everything was finished.

Wow... just look at our sukkah now! I could really imagine a family sitting at the table enjoying a holiday meal.

Of course, I was one of the winners! It was really something to see my sukkah on the display with my name attached to it. It was the best one on the table! Everyone agreed! It remained on view for the entire week of

Sukkot. I received a bracelet with a mezuzah on it for my prize.

The real prize for me had been just one more pure fun encounter with my brother. In each one he had been generous to me and sweet and patient. I always stood by his side in awe of his imagination and creativity, talents that I lacked. I wanted to emulate him. He was my best big brother!

Bedtime, 1957

I SHARE MY bedroom with my big sister Jo Ann...who goes to sleep way after I do. So I climb into my single bed that is next to the window. My bed barely has room in it for me as I collect stuffed animals and must sleep with all of them to get a good night's sleep.

Zippy, a monkey that Martin bought me is my favorite of all of the animals. He is so realistic with a tee shirt, pants and white sneakers. Zippy has become one of my confidantes and holds many of my secrets and my worries. I take Zippy to my chest, settle in and call: "Mommy I am ready now for you to put me to bed." The nighttime routine is that my mother comes and sits with me and we review the day together and then I get my kiss goodnight. This is my one special time alone with my Mom and I treasure it. With her kiss and all of my buddies I am ready to go to sleep with ease.

Mommy scoots onto the little bit of space on the side of my bed and gives me a goodnight hug.

Now it is review time:

"Mommy, why was daddy so angry again with Martin? Martin really is so sweet why can't Daddy ever see it? Look at me and my bed... all of these soft friends love Martin... and some of them he even brought home for me. He is not such a bad guy as daddy thinks he is."

"I know you worry about him all of the time," mother says. "It's not your worry it's for daddy and me to be concerned about him."

"But mommy this happens all of the time and I think that he has no one in his corner."

"Fredi, I have to tell you this with all honesty. I am in his corner everyday... and it might seem weird for me to tell you this but I love him the most of my three children. Please understand when I say this that it does not mean that I love you less... but he needs my love more than you do or Jo Ann does. Because he has always had problems he has my heart with him every minute of every day... and I know that you do not need this focus from me... that you are just fine on your own."

I reassured my mother... I knew exactly what she was sharing... and I knew she was right. He needed more of her love to help him be okay... even though it didn't seem to be working out so well.

I told her, "Mommy don't worry that you said this to me. I understand. If you need to love him more please do so. I love him and it makes me feel better to know that you love him so much. I think you are right. He needs more of you than Jo Ann and I do... we seem to be doing okay after all... so give him enough so that he will be better. I want him to be better!

"That's my Fredi... I knew I could say that to you and you would understand! I love you for who you are every day my daughter... now time for that goodnight kiss! "

And then off to sleep.

Zippy will be by my side to help me understand if I still need to talk about this.

Thanks Martin for buying me my friend Zippy!

Pleasant dreams.

Oh no, here we go

SUNDAYS WERE THE times that either mother made a scrumptious dinner at home or we would go out for a special dinner at a restaurant… a luxury for my mother to have the day completely at leisure and a meal out.

One Sunday we were told that we would go out to dinner to the "Pub" restaurant in Cherry Hill New Jersey. In the late afternoon all of us began our preparations for this outing. We all tumbled into the Buick in our Sunday finery… me in my favorite wool sweater and skirt with patent leather Mary-Janes… and Jo Ann dressed in a similar fashion. When Martin came down the steps ready to go there might already have been tension in the air.

My father immediately noticed that Martin had slicked his hair back with too much grease in it, looking not clean cut and respectable like he should have looked to go out for fancy dinner. Mother interceded on his behalf to assure that as we got into the car we were at peace as a family… that war had not already ensued… the dinner was a treat after all. Mother always took Martin's part and tried to find a way to get my father to calm down.

The Pub was in South Jersey and so we had about a forty minute drive from home to get there. The "in the car dialogue" would have included these directions from my father:

"While this is a special night out please be reasonable in what you order for dinner. There are plenty of things on the menu that are not exorbitantly priced and I would appreciate it if you ordered them so that tonight's dinner will be affordable for our family."

It was always way too busy at the Pub on Sundays and this day was no different. It seems like many families had the same idea and a usual wait of over an hour for a table was normal. Our family sat waiting by a cozy fireplace smelling steaks grilling and working up an appetite.

After an hour we sat down, and did not really even have to look at the menu as we knew from many previous visits what we were "allowed" to order and what was out of our price category. So Jo Ann and I ordered first, and stuck with the program. When the waitress came to Martin here is what transpired:

"Well I will have the Shrimp cocktail first and then the Filet Mignon medium rare for my main course."

Oh no here we go.

This was not supposed to happen after my father's lecture. But Martin had other ideas, obviously

My father looked at him in silent fury... and my mother grabbed my father's arm and implored him with a silent look not to make a scene... just let it go... let Martin have what Martin wanted... and her silent look conveyed that she would order the lesser items to compensate.

We all knew that he should never have done that... but we all wanted to keep the peace and not have this meal devolve into a Hess family war... so we ate in silence... and Martin gloated in his small victory. He relished every bite of his dinner. For the rest of us, once the order was entered it was hard to enjoy the dinner or the night out as the preoccupation about what would ensue later spoiled the food and the ambiance.

In my own silence I knew well that all hell would break loose once we were in the car and on the way home and that the hell would not abate at home either. Perhaps this would be one of those times that my father pushed Martin down the cellar steps in anger. What started out as a pleasant family outing ended in sadness for everyone... except perhaps, for Martin.

I never understood as a child why these things continued to happen in just this same fashion. Why did my father issue rules in that way? Why did Martin hear the rules as an invitation to rebel? Why couldn't we be like other families and just go out to dinner? Why did Martin keep putting himself in situations that could only end poorly for him and for all of us?

Dinner at home just may be worse

SUNDAY MORNING DAWNS bright in our kitchen at 1119 Barringer Street. After the breakfast dishes are all washed and put away. My mother begins her most prized activity, preparing for a Sunday dinner at home.

While she is in the kitchen my father is in the living room reading the New York Times and watching "Meet the Press." He is studying up on all worldly topics as possible discussion for the family dinner for all of us.

Mother cooks all day. The house has delicious smells wafting through every room…with savory and sweet mixing together. By the afternoon she is finished all of her preparations and she and my father sneak away for a "Sunday nap"…which I later came to understand was their time to be intimate with each other, even though Jo Ann, Martin and I might be lurking somewhere in the house while they were "napping."

So when it was dinner time both of my parents emerged well rested and satisfied and should have been in the place that would allow for a warm and peaceful dinner for the five of us. I invite you now to the table.

The dining room in our house was a formal dining room with a dining room set with five chairs around the wooden table and a breakfront, a sideboard and a smaller dresser as part of the set. The seating for dinner did not vary. Mother sat at the end of the table closest to the kitchen so that she could bring her bounty to the table. Martin and I sat on one side of the table… me closest to my mother and he, closest to my father. Jo Ann sat across from us and my father sat at the head of the table that was in front of the breakfront.

My mother brought the Shrimp Lamaze to the table as the first course with a delicious tossed salad. Why her salad was the best salad I ever ate, I still am not really sure, but even both of my daughters remember and comment on her salad when they remember dinner at their grandparents apartment many years later. Dinner generally began peacefully and then could rapidly devolve in to anger and harsh words. My father would take off on telling all of us that he knew that a particular politician was all wrong in his approach. If there was any chance that someone might question his wisdom, trouble would ensue.

He routinely directed his political insights first to Jo Ann who he deemed the only one at the table capable of understanding his viewpoint and engaging with him in a meaningful dialogue. My sister had adopted a similar style of argumentation as my father's and if their voices began to rise in vehement discourse all was okay... because my father liked this type of debate and respected Jo Ann for her ability to keep up with him. During these forays, Martin, my mother and I generally stayed pretty much out of the fray.

But oh no stupid little Fredi had accidently spilled her water all over the table during the debate! Now the anger erupted: "There she goes again. Can't you sit at the table and behave without making such a stupid mess," my father would scream at me. By now, he was banging on the table and his face was crimson ... over spilled water!

I was and I am a crier and so the tears came easily which only made him angrier. "Oh now she is crying. Can't you take me getting angry when I should be angry at you? Do you have to subject all of us to your sniveling?"

If I even tried to answer and tell my father that if I could control my tears, I would, that would only make it worse... and eventually he would send me to finish my dinner in the kitchen for my combination of spilling water and crying over it. (You mustn't cry over spilled milk took on a different meaning in the Hess family)

While exiled in the kitchen I would overhear now my mother's plaintive voice trying to talk my father down off his angry harangue... as they continued to eat the prime rib of beef with all of the accoutrements.

Mother would entreat my father, "Please Sam just forget about the whole thing and let's have a pleasant Sunday evening as a family." Her efforts were useless The more she tried the angrier he became, and my father most likely had my very intelligent sensitive mother also on the verge of tears. Martin to the rescue! Martin was then able to do or say something so inflammatory that my water spill seemed ridiculous. I know that whatever he did was not accidental. Martin would not sit by and allow my father to demean my mother. He could see how out of proportion my father 's anger had been towards me and my mother and he knew he could "take my father on." And so he did. And now things would get really ugly really fast. Martin would incite my father to grab him physically in anger... something he never did with his daughters. My father's seat was right next to the door to the recreation room downstairs... and their angry words might end in he and Martin pushing one another... and Martin landing at the bottom of the recreation room steps. Martin never showed any emotion in these altercations and if my father pushed him down the steps... Martin would never even give him the satisfaction of crying or admitting to physical pain.

Meanwhile, Jo Ann sat at the table an observer, she the only one to get off scot free. She quietly ate her dinner in the methodical way she always did... one vegetable at a time... and finally the main course... she never ate things together... just one at a time... and slowly.

Eventually, after all of the tumult was over... we would slink back to the table... even me the one in the kitchen—and the meal would continue in silence. The food was always delicious and could drown a bit of the upset. Perhaps by the time we got to the home-made chocolate cake and parfait we were talking again... about nothing of import. But we all also felt some disquiet in the pit of our stomachs... all of this sturm and drang over really nothing at all.

What just happened? Why is Daddy always so angry? Why is the smallest thing so incendiary for him? How can I live my life perfectly so that I am never the one to make him so enraged? Why is Martin always so willing and able to take the rap for these incidents?

When we left the table and all went back to our own corners (homework up in my bedroom or TV), I think we all knew that if we asked my father what had happened at dinner that night he would have told a story about what Martin did to make him so angry.

By then, he would have forgotten that what started it all is that Fredi had spilled her water. Even he could see on reflection how ridiculous that might have sounded.

And there was Martin to his left, smirking at him knowingly. The war between them was constant... and there was no one seemingly able to stop it.

Guilt again on my part as I drifted off to sleep that night. chastising myself for knocking over my water glass and thus starting the physical match between my father and my brother at such times my heart ached for Martin and I felt only confused about and fearful of my father.

I will try harder next week.

Dream house, 1957

THE YEAR BEFORE my brother's Bar Mitzvah our family made several important changes. My parents opened their own business in Northeast Philadelphia, Tacony Curtain and Linen store. In order to be able to buy this business my parents sold the house on 18th Street in East Oak Lane. This necessitated our move to 8405 Williams Ave in West Oak Lane. This house was a row house that our family rented.

I believe that both of these developments were not pleasing to my mother. She did not want to be the CEO of a curtain and linen store. My father, the "big businessman," left all the real running of that business to her as he maintained his job with the wholesale linen company, Silver Dry Goods. In this position my father was able to continue to be out on the street schmoozing with his clients while my mother was back at the real source of income running the operation. And my mother hated the house! To her, it was a come down. The house was small, and had not one distinctive quality to it. The neighborhood was made up of street after street of the same house as our house. I think she also believed that the people living in this area were less sophisticated than she hoped to be. In every regard her life was different than she could have envisioned... except for the time when she was with her children... which was less than she wanted as she worked every day but Saturday and Sunday, at the store.

After several years of living in the hated row house, there was an interesting raffle that was taking place in sprawling suburban Cheltenham Township, for a dream house! That was how they advertised it..."Win Your Dream

House." We went to see the house and enter the raffle. The house was a split level near the mall that was being built. It was everything that we could have imagined... or dreamed of! It had every new convenience and a beautiful yard and patio. It had four bathrooms and a recreation room... and oh the kitchen... my mother could have created such artistry in that kitchen! Ironically, the chimney of the house sported a Large Cursive "L" on the outside. We all took it as a sign that we would actually win the house... as my mother's name, Lucille was imprinted on it. We filled out the raffle and waited, sure that our dream would come true.

Meanwhile, another easier-to-attain dream house

DURING THAT FIRST year in the row house my mother saw an ad in one of her women's magazines for "Plans to build a dream dollhouse" and ordered them.

When the plans arrived my mother shared them with Martin and I and asked if we had interest in them. Of course I did, and fortunately so did he, as he would be the builder of this Dream House. Martin studied the plans and made a list of the supplies that would be needed to build the house including the tools as there were no tools in the Hess family before this project. I have no idea how Martin knew how to construct something of wood with nails. What did he know of saws, hammers and levels?

Every night after dinner, he and I would escape to the garage to work on the project. My job was simply to keep him company each night as he built the house. I watched the split level single home develop right before my eyes. It was so very "contemporary" and was the type of home that only "rich" people were able to afford. This house was similar to the Dream House we had entered the raffle for! Once the structure was complete Martin required me to leave him alone in the garage. With the house up and standing it was now time for him to decorate it... and all of this he wanted as a final surprise for me.

He stained the outside of the house a burnt wooden color and the window frames and the front door were painted white. Each room in the house was wall-papered with a different pattern. He found something that resembled tile to put on the bathroom floor and a faux linoleum for the kitchen. He used terry cloth towels to substitute for carpeting. Wash clothes were used to make wall-to-wall carpeting. He invited my mother into the project only to buy the furniture for each of the rooms.

By Hanukah of that year, the Dream House was completed and furnished and ready for me. I loved that house! It transported me daily to the world of those "rich" people and the way they lived. My dollhouse family was part of the world that we were striving for in my family... and my brother had been able to create that world for me. We never did win the raffle on the real house... this house would have to suffice for me for now.

The house remained standing in my room for several years. Then one year, my cousin Cindy, had her tonsils out and became quite ill. My mother asked my cousin Joyce if she thought the dollhouse would help in Cindy's recovery. Without my knowing, the house was delivered to Cindy for her get well gift from us.. When I heard that she was better .I asked my mother if I could have my house back.

I was told: "No, we cannot ask for the house back from them... once you give a gift it is a gift and you cannot expect to have it returned."

So just as mother "lost her Dream House"... mine too would be lost to me... just a memory now.

At least for a little while... Martin had assured that someone had a "Dream House."

"We are allowed to do this": A lesson learned at Penn Fruit

SATURDAY MORNING, NO shul this week as Martin, Jo Ann and I are joining mother to do the weekly grocery shopping. We all loved going to the Penn Fruit on Ogontz Ave. It was quite an adventure.

We all pile into the mint green Buick with the dark green top and green leather seats—quite a spiffy car for that time—and off we go for the market.

As soon as we get inside mother and I go one way and Martin and Jo Ann seem content to wander off on their own. I have no idea why they are not staying with mother and me. What I so loved about the marketing was being with my mother and having her teach me why she chose the items that she put in the basket. This is our time together and it is alright with us that the "other two" have disappeared.

I also loved that the Penn Fruit has samples of new items to try, a bit like having hors d'oeuvres throughout the market.

As we pull into the candy aisle we spot them happily having their own adventure.

I would learn from Jo Ann that Martin taught her that you go to this aisle and that aisle and look for "open" packages and then the "rule" is that you can help yourself to however much you want. He explained to my sister that the market "allowed" this and actually understood that customers would sample from open packages.

I doubt that this was ever true, and further I suspect that the packages that were sampled from might not always have been already "opened."

I told my sister that I "did not approve" of this practice and would not eat the candy that she had pointed out to me as free. This time it was a small ice cream cone with a marshmallow in the place of the ice cream. I actually loved this treat but I would not take part in this part of the marketing adventure.

I am sure Jo Ann let Martin know that the little "judge" had determined that their practice was not "kosher" and that I would not be a part of it.

This was just one of those times that the youngest sibling was just a pain in the butt... always there to remind them that their good time was illicit...

"Ok suit yourself you little baby... stick by mother... like you always do... and we will have candy... and you will have none! It's really no fun to go to the market with you!"

They were a pair. I was the outsider in this particular venture. When things crossed the line in their activities they knew I could be counted on to opt out.

Some things in this episode say quite a bit about how life will unfold... in the coming years.

According to Martin, the owners of the market "let you have all of that candy"

In my heart I knew that this was not true.

Sunday night trouble

MY PARENTS OFTEN went out on Sunday nights. As soon as they were out of sight, Martin would come up with a plan. Often we would play "restaurant." He was the chef and my sister was the waitress, I was the customer. These roles never changed. So my sister would "take my order" but... I really did not get to choose what I would be eating that night. I distinctly remember one menu that I was served. It consisted of a can of Le Sueur peas with an entire stick of butter melted into it... a drink of orange juice, crème de menthe syrup and chocolate syrup and tuna fish mixed with jelly. My sister would serve it to me and then the chef would come to the table to see that I ate it! And the commentary was always the same: "the food is actually delicious that way... and you better eat it because I used up good food in preparing it... and if you don't eat it... you! you will get in trouble as I will tell the parents that you made me make it that way for you. "The other warning that was always issued was quite universal... never tell that we have these escapades as then the parents won't let him be in charge of us anymore.

One night our "game" caused us to break the "reflector's" glass. There was a lamp that stood in the corner of the living room... and we were always warned not to "break the reflector"... well we did it this time! The trick was how to get the glass cleaned up... and a replacement glass in its place before the parents returned home. I believe that instead we "cooked up" the story of how the reflector innocently was broken... and I am not sure I remember how... and who was deemed the guilty one... but I am pretty sure it had not been my brother! We all knew that if he was found at fault all hell would break loose between my father and Martin... and Martin would probably be beaten by my father if he was found guilty. I am sure I preferred to be the one to break it... as I was the baby... and I was often spared the fury my father could display quite easily.

One perfect night: Fun and business

HALLOWEEN WAS ALL Martin all of the time! He was not so into the costume... but he was very into Trick or Treat. This year that I recall, Martin was in his usual costume... his "hoodlum" attire... his black leather jacket and black pants with some make-up that made him look tough. My sister... was in her usual outfit as well... she was dressed as a bum, and I wore my clown pajamas as my costume.

We headed out together right after dinner and Martin dictated the route we would follow. He was pretty definite about the fact that we had to go to every single house on those six streets and then the "best" stores on Wadsworth Ave that had the best candy of all. He was extremely excited about Halloween and wanted to make sure we stuck to his plan. That was a lot of houses to cover in just about four hours... it was also an enormous amount of candy to carry!

We were not able to make this trip in one circuit. It would require that we return home several times during the night to empty our bags onto the dining room table. I can hear my own voice imploring Martin to allow me to skip the next trip out... and his response assuring that to do so would be to miss the very best part of the evening. So as much as I had grown exhausted I would have pulled up my last ounce of strength and go out yet one more time with Martin and JoAnn. He was right of course. Had I not gone out that last time I would have missed the store that was giving out the giant candy bars... or the house that gave out Apple Taffies. The three of us were quite sure that we had amassed the best collection of anyone in our neighborhood. This would be confirmed on our return home as we saw the mountain of candy we had garnered. It was massive.

Generally, Martin would convince my parents that he had to remain home from school the next day... he was "not feeling well." What actually was on his mind was the stash that we had collected. He would spend that next day categorizing the items gleaned. I am sure that this process included what candy he deemed worthy of keeping... and then what candy he might be able to sell to someone. This pure fun...would also be a business venture for him. My sister and I were just content to have spent that entire night with him... amassing this mountain of candy... and then claiming some of it for ourselves. We were fully willing for him to have his "business" with some of the spoils.

Pauline and Eddie's

PICTURE THIS PLACE. It's on the corner of Wadsworth Avenue and Forrest Ave . It's in the basement of one of the many identical row houses in this very middle class neighborhood. It's a luncheonette. I was inside the store probably only once.

It has a candy counter by the register and a counter to sit at to order lunch. In the back of the store are pinball machines. The odor is redolent of greasy Philadelphia cheese steaks and onions. The lighting is poor and so the entire store has a dark overcast to it... it set the mood for mystery.

Why was I only inside once? After all, it was just across the street from our house.

The characters that frequented it were greasy -haired, tough looking, black leather motorcycle jacket wearing guys. Everything about them announced, "trouble."

If I wanted candy... I would just walk all the way up further on Wadsworth Ave to another candy store... Dairy Made where it was shiny, bright clean and safe!

While I avoided the possibility of entry into the inner sanctum of Pauline and Eddie's, Martin was drawn to it like a magnet.

We were told by our parents that we were not to go there." The people who go into that store are not like us. They most likely are not even Jewish!"

Yet the words of prohibition, warning of our differences were exactly what drew Martin there. If those guys smoked Lucky Strike cigarettes then Martin began to smoke them too... if they listened to funky music, black soul music and performers that were unknown to the rest of us... then that was what he most liked... if they dressed like thugs... then he would too.

Martin hung out with these guys... but I doubt that they were ever really like "friends." He learned from them all of the tricks of the trade, but not a one of them ever entered our house. Martin never named any of them to my sister or me.

This was probably his first foray into having a group of men that he congregated with and schemed with... but did not really belong with.

Real friends, were somehow not so important to him. It was enough for Martin to be invited into the darkness of Pauline and Eddies... and mimic the guys that inhabited it...

He could dream there of being one of them... not one of us!

What makes Martin run

HOW OFTEN WERE my parents asked if they understood that Martin was different, and not in a good way?

When Martin was in Elementary School at Logan Demonstration School the teachers and administrators wondered why this bright little boy was doing so poorly. He was tested and my parents were told that he was quite bright and should be equally capable. Yet they were witnessing little evidence of his brightness. He had the prerequisite skills... he could read and write and do mathematics but he was never interested in putting any effort into anything that was asked of him. He rarely did the homework that was assigned. In the meeting in which this information was shared with my parents everyone determined that Martin willfully shirked anything that was asked of him. And so it began, the labels... he was just difficult... he was bad... and everyone agreed about this.

Another opinion

I WAS OFTEN sick when I was growing up and as a result I spent a great deal of time visiting Dr. Lowenberg's Pediatric practice. On one of these visits after my "current infection" was diagnosed and the shot of penicillin was administered my mother asked the doctor if she could have a few minutes time to discuss another matter with him.

I was asked to leave the room and she and Dr. Lowenberg had time to talk. On our way home I asked my mother what she needed this private time with him about...was there something more wrong with me that she could not discuss in front of me? No... my mother reassured me... it was not me, what I suffered from was easy to cure... she needed to talk with the doctor about Martin.

So what had the doctor suggested to her about what was "wrong" with Martin? She related to me that the doctor had suggested that Martin see a child psychiatrist and talk with this doctor about the problems that he seemed to have in school and socially. Finally, I could relax. Someone who knew these types of problems well would be able to help my brother and thus help all of us.

My mother discussed this with my father and my brother and an appointment was made with the recommended psychiatrist. Martin was not happy to be going, as he told my parents that there was nothing wrong with him. He was just different than what they expected. But he went. The appointments did not last for long as after several sessions my brother refused to go anymore. He promised that he would try harder on his own to act more conventional...

and that the doctor could not help him. As he said before, he thought he was "just fine" as he was.

My parents were actually relieved by this. They felt that Martin had gotten the message and that from there on it would be smooth sailing. I couldn't have been any older than eight or nine years old... and yet I was unhappy to learn that my parents so easily gave up on this doctor. My mother tried to reassure me that Martin now promised that he would be "better"... and that it would be a pure waste of money for him to see a psychiatrist if he really did not need one. I wanted to believe this to be true but it did not add up for me If it was so easy for Martin to just change and act consistently the way everyone wanted him to...why had he not done so up until now?

I think my parents just wanted to believe that it was in his power to change... and that he was "normal" and not in need of help (this was in an era in which psychotherapy was pretty much taboo, so his few visits in and of themselves were novel). This began a well-rehearsed pattern with Martin of acknowledging an issue, trying to deal with it and then ultimately hoping that it had magically gone away.

Shortly after the end of the psychiatrist's visits my mother learned that one of their closest social friends had sent their son off to a military boarding school to help him to be able to "get with the program," and were very pleased with the results. So my mother got all of the paperwork from that school and wanted desperately for my brother to have a chance to go there. My father let her know that this was a "pipedream"... there was no way that the family could finance this type of extravagance. Martin would just have to right his course on his own.

A foray at Camp Maribel: The warning issued yet again

MY SISTER AND I had been campers at a small summer camp just an hour from home. For both of us this camp was heaven on earth. It was extremely unconventional, with just about 80 campers and no emphasis on sports! At this camp I always felt that whoever I was to be celebrated and it was the same for every single camper. Some of the things that campers did here were hilariously funny and at any other camp would be seen as "weird."

The summer when I was ten years old my brother joined us at camp. As he was older, and a teen, he was spending the summer as a "waiter." He and his fellow waiters served all of the food for the three meals and then they were free to enjoy the camp and its activities. The waiters lived in a small cabin across the road from the main campus.

Somehow Martin assembled materials to make the waiters cabin into a "destination." He decorated it, built a barbecue pit outside of the cabin, .and then found chairs and umbrellas to create a lounge by the barbecue. He also found a way to have music playing--quite loudly--to broadcast a show that could be heard throughout the camp. He would invite others "up to the cabin" to witness all that was going on there. He had also found a way to confiscate enough hotdogs etc. to use the barbecue pit he had built... and maybe even charge for the refreshments.

My parents often came up to the camp for an evening ride. During one visit, the camp director and camp owners shared with my parents "how unusual" they found my brother's creativity to be,. and not in the best way. They explained that while his escapades often started out as fun--.and exciting for the other waiters--they had gotten out of hand and they had had to put a stop to them. (Where have we heard this song before?). The camp director told my parents that he found my brother to be akin to the character "Sammy Glick" from the novel *What Makes Sammy Run*. His tremendous creative drive to get ahead or to do what others were not could cause someone to feel that he had been stabbed in the back. The director felt he had to firmly share this information with my parents as this behavior needed to be dealt with immediately, or he could predict that something unfortunate was possible for Martin.

So yet again, my parents heard this message, and by summer's end, when he was back at home, they shoved it aside and hoped that it would go away.

It is so hard to accept that others knew and had tried to intervene... that suggestions were made and weakly tried... that we never really grasped the problem and dealt with it. I don't know if it was a feeling of impotence, ignorance, or wishful thinking that caused this approach.

It has always had me wondering that if any of these pieces of information had had a different impact could all of this have turned out differently?

The root of all evil

MY BROTHER BEGAN working at my parents' linen shop on weekends right after his Bar Mitzvah. At the same time, he got a job working at a dry cleaning shop after school several days of the week. This began a pattern for him... of juggling life... juggling always several jobs... and devoting himself very little to what most boys his age would be attracted to, like school, and sports and proper socializing. Even at this young age he would come home from both jobs with his head spinning with ideas. He was always sure that he actually knew how to run a business better than my father and mother... and better than the owner of the dry cleaner. The cleaner was impressed with how hard he worked and the enthusiasm he brought to his work. He also loved that my brother was offering him suggestions for how to make his business more appealing. Martin would tell him: "Why not have special days when if you brought just sweaters to the cleaner you would get a special deal!" and "Why not sell candy from the counter so that the customers could get a snack when they came to pick up their clothing!" His drive in this way was insatiable.

Eventually, after he was a bit older, he was able to convince my parents that they could make a lot more money if only they followed his plan. He worked like this at such a young age because he always wanted money in his pocket to be able to buy gifts for those he loved, and to do the "things" he should not be doing, that none of us understood. I cannot be sure of what the transgressions were at that time. Perhaps just little things then like buying the verboten cigarettes and sleazy looking clothing. He often came home from the dry cleaner with a new toy for me... usually another stuffed animal. He went into the women's shop next door to the cleaner... the Shelley Shoppe and he bought my mother a new blouse or even a dress. He knew her size and he wanted to please her always. When Martin came home bearing gifts you could not help but love him for it. He also brought the stories home from his many jobs. He was excited that he had been able to improve the dry cleaners in whatever way he had dreamed up that week. He also loved the positive feedback that this brought to him from the owner. While he bragged about his accomplishments, I know that in my upwardly striving home, they were not really valued. My parents had the expectations that all middle class Jewish parents had in the 1950's that their children would reach above the station that they were born into. In my family that meant to get far away from any retail endeavor... as they saw "the business" as a constant headache that never yielded all that they aspired to. For my mother in particular, that meant a dream for academic excellence and a profession, her own unfulfilled pathway.

So the accomplishments that Martin consistently offered were half-heartedly accepted... and he knew it. He also knew that my sister and I were more likely to adhere to the dreams that my mother still held onto.

Martin ultimately had a vision for a custom drapery business that he convinced my parents to embrace. The store remained downstairs and the upstairs became a mini-factory with seamstresses making the draperies. My mother was running both of these businesses, with help from my brother and father. She actually was the brains behind this operation. My brother was the main salesman. He would go to people's homes and measure and design... and promise them the moon. His creative drive had this little operation over-extended all of the time. My mother worked tirelessly to try to deliver all that the customers had been promised... and on time. It was a constant source of stress. The family business was now way bigger that anyone had imagined possible and at times was even making more money. Unfortunately, there were also too many times when the order was incorrect and had to be done again... and there were often very unhappy customers. It was also the place where my parents and my brother fought the most. Martin had pushed them to expand for him... and at times he would absent himself from this expansion. When he would reappear (and they often did not know where he had vanished to) he did not want to hear about things that were problematic. This was a set-up for him to explosively interact... mainly with my mother... but when it was also with my father... it turned ugly very fast. My mother was willing to absorb so much of his acting out because she loved Martin intensely... and she just wanted him to be okay. So she would be the sponge for all his shenanigans. At some point, Martin got bored with the family drapery business and moved on to start his own businesses.

From my research, I have learned Martin had a custom drapery business with some of the people he was involved with in the drug smuggling business. At the same time, he had a carpet business that was based in several different marketplaces... one in Pennsauken New Jersey and one in South Philadelphia. And with all of this, he would at times drop back into the family drapery business for short bursts of time Clearly he was also involved then with organized crime. He had so many balls in the air at the same time it is even dizzying to write about it. This coming from my brother, who vowed to me that he did not want to work as hard as our parents to make a buck. I am sure that he believed that his involvement in crime was going to be his ticket out. It would be in its own perverse manner.

He gave me a road to the "cool crowd"

I SPENT A great deal of time growing up doing things on my own. Jo Ann and I shared a room but we were mainly opposites.

She was studious... I really did not care so much about school... I always did well enough without any effort at all.

She was an athlete... playing basketball, tennis... anything with a ball and she was very good at it... I could not connect with a ball if my life depended upon it.

She always had her head in a book, .I was always playing with dolls and stuffed animals.

She hated anything to do with cooking. I loved every minute in the kitchen.

So she and I were not a pair, and did not really become close until we were adults.

Martin was another story. If he invited me in I ran to be a part of his plan. His plan was always exotic and forbidden and generally had little relationship to anything I would do on my own, nerd, do-gooder and goody two shoes that I was.

Invitations included:

1. "Let's decorate the walls in my bedroom before we leave this house at 8405 Williams Ave." I knew that this idea was not a good one but he was persuasive. "The new tenants will like it better after we get done with it... the way it is now is so boring!"

And so I would join him standing on his bed marking all of the walls with painted designs and scenes. When our parents returned home they were horrified at what we had done to his room, sure that they would have to pay a painter to repair the damage, and there was no money for that.

2."I have to go out to WIBG to meet with Hy Lit...why don't you come with me." What could be a better invitation than this one for a teenager when I was growing up? WIBG was the station that I listened to... and Hy Lit was famous! He was the disc jockey that everyone who was cool listened to! If I went with my brother I would have stories to tell in the lunchroom the next day at school that would buy me favor with the "cooler crowd."

So off I went with my brother to the studio... and I sat and watched the "stars" do their thing. Martin sat with Hy Lit and the two of them planned their next show which would take place at a drive- in movie theater. They discussed at length who the stars would be at the concert and how the stage would be set up. It might have been Connie Francis—a big catch for the two of them! I could not wait to brag about it the next day. I loved seeing Martin in his element. He seemed so knowledgeable about all that needed to happen so that the "act" could be a success. I did not know how he had learned all that he knew, he frankly amazed me. And the stars all listened to him. They hung on his every word, deferring to him as the expert—my brother. The stars loved him and I did too!

I loved Martin for taking me outside of my cocoon. He was so cool and with it in every way that I was not. On the trip home in his car I asked so many questions about all of the famous people that he had encountered and how he had gotten in with such important people. He had me so envious that he was so much more than I could ever even think of being. I let him know that I thought there was no one else like him in my life, because of course there wasn't!

And there were more invitations, so many more...

He brought me to a rock concert that he organized-- that was much more impressive than the trip to WIBG because at this concert not only Hy Lit and Jerry Blavat were present but so many of the important acts that were popular then: the Shirelles, Connie Francis--really anyone who was important to 1960's teenagers in Philadelphia. He had booked them and brought them to the theater .He interacted with them directly and he brought me with him... backstage!

Martin took me to places that I never would have gone without him. My first trip to the Latin Casino, a supper club in New Jersey, was with Martin. It was glamorous and had the most up to the minute shows. I might be able to be there when Frank Sinatra was on stage! Martin paid my way, sat with me and encouraged me to have the "best food" on the menu. Barbra Streisand was the new up and coming star in the musical "Funny Girl." When it came to Philadelphia Martin and I went to see it together. We left the theater that night aware that we had both just witnessed a force to be reckoned with.

By the time I graduated high school all of this involvement with Martin stopped... I had moved on now to fulfill the script that I had been offered as a middle class Jewish girl... go to college to meet that "prince charming"... preferably a pre-professional... even better a doctor... and while you are at it learn a little too...

We were not to regain that closeness in the ensuing years... and I learned that he had found not only all of the "stars" but the underworld too. Perhaps that was why his work with Hy Lit came to an end during this period too. As was Martin's way,, he just moved on. He offered no explanation to us about why he was moving on... it was just "new opportunities" had opened up for him.

I searched for my man... and found him. Martin found his men too.

A balanced scale

I AM ENVISIONING the scale that we used in Chemistry class that had two pans… one on each side that weighed the chemicals needed for an experiment. It was important to get the two pans to align with each other, and to do so with great care. If one pan tipped too far in a negative direction… the entire balance would be thrown off and the chemical process would not work out at all. The experiment would definitely fail.

Why this particular picture?

I think that my brother and I were like those two pans on the scales. He was the negative force and I was the positive force and together we could continue to keep the family in balance… as long as we remained well connected. When Martin did something that caused an issue… which he consistently did… I knew it was up to me then to do something to "fix it"… to get the two pans of the scale back in alignment.

I remember one year… around Mother's Day my brother had been particularly difficult with my mother. In fact, I saw that one day she came home from the store with a swelling on her face. When I asked her what had happened she quietly confessed to me that she and Martin had gotten into a disagreement… most likely about some aspect of his life or his appearance that she could not countenance. In the heat of the argument, he had hit my mother in the face. She then assured me that Martin immediately felt horrible about what had happened and apologized profusely. Mother had no idea about why things got so out of hand so quickly. (It now seems that even then Martin had gotten himself involved with very dangerous people. Perhaps my mother's words had awakened some fear in him that caused him to react so violently to the person he loved most in our family... mother.)

The scales... they were completely out of balance... I heard the heartbreak in mother's voice as she confessed the days altercation to me.

What could I do? I needed to act swiftly to bring my mother some happiness and some peace.

So the next day, on the way to Hebrew School I got off of the bus a stop early so that I could stop at a jewelry store on my way. I took all of the money that I had stashed away with me and hoped that it would be enough to buy something beautiful for my Mother. Something that would immediately reduce the swelling near her eye... but really mend the crack that was made in her heart.

I found a pin that was made of gold and garnets in a circle. I could afford it! It would be perfect... mother would love it.

Though it was not yet Mother's Day, I could not save it until then. I needed to give it to her immediately that night when I got home from Hebrew School.

At dinner, I handed her the beautifully wrapped package and watched as she opened it and the obvious joy that gesture brought to my mother. She exclaimed: "What is this for? Where did you get it?"

I explained that I had gotten off the bus one stop early in search of a gift for her... just because... I wanted to buy her something of beauty... "because you are the best mother on earth!"

I could not say that I was trying to balance the scales... I don't even know that I consciously understood then what I was doing. I had learned well though that I had this gift... this ability to see the other and think of what could ameliorate a difficult situation. Martin had thrown the scale off so badly... but I thought I could level it out a bit... and I did.

The result was that my eye was always focused on the scale... and focused on assuring that it stayed as level as I could make it. While we all still lived at home this was possible... in small ways.

But I never did stop trying. That was my job in the family.

And still we were loved

NOT ALWAYS UNDERSTOOD, but loved.

It hit me as I discussed growing up with my husband on the occasion of his birthday that his growing up experience was very different from mine... in his there were rarely:

- Birthday cards, presents or parties
- Hanukah presents or celebration
- Jewish holidays marked with family gatherings
- Special meals at the formal dinner table
- Long talks about feelings
- Reflections about the goings on in the world
- Friends welcomed into the home

In my house all of the above were regular occurrences... many initiated by my mother but some also by my father. So in the midst of the "issue" of my brother and his problems and a lack of insight about what to do about them... there resided a sense of family love and deep connection.

My mother always knew what her children wanted and made sure that we got it.

I can vividly describe birthday parties that she had planned for me... even down to the menu that she prepared... and cherished gifts that were a part of the celebration.

When I was twelve years old my mother planned a fancy "dinner party" for me and my friends. It was all very grown up… in the dining room. It was a turkey dinner with all of the fixings… and the beautiful homemade birthday cake. I recall my brother acting as waiter for the party and he helped to make it festive. Martin was that waiter that really doted on each "customer." He would ask if the meal was sufficient and would suggest that if anything else was needed, he was the one to ask. He really put on the affect of a fancy waiter. Unfortunately, I was harboring an illness that I tried very hard to keep under wraps until the party's end… but it was clear that I was feverish… and my friends did wind up leaving early. By the time all had left I was burning up with fever… and within hours we realized that we had exposed all of my friends to the measles.

After that party I was the sickest I had ever been. My fever raged for days and my mother… the nurse remained awake for all of those days painting all of the "paint by number" oil paintings that one of my friends gave me as a gift. She was too afraid to allow herself to sleep as I was at times delirious with high fever. She never once complained about having to sit by my bedside night after night.

I was loved… we were loved…

The gifts always met the needs of the child.

For Jo Ann it was sporting equipment.

For Martin it was flashy jewelry that my mother did not personally like, but he did, so it was a star sapphire pinky ring, or a diamond ring or a gold flashy watch.

For me it was generally the latest doll, book or jewelry.

We had family traditions like for the tenth birthday… each of us got our first real watch… and we got to choose it.

So there was happiness and celebration in the house… that accompanied the tension… and I believe this carried me solidly through my formative years. I really felt like my family was a warm and good family to be a part of.

But the happiness and celebration also allowed us to forget that there was a bigger topic being ignored.

Hanukah, 1958

I SAW THAT same commercial every single day on TV for a new doll, "Poor Pitiful Pearl."

She came with a story of Rags to Riches... dressed in her clothes that were to make her look like a "poor, indigent" child... and with one or two outfits that would transform her into the rich version of Pearl. One night when all of us were watching TV the ad for Pearl came on, and I beseeched: "Mommy it would really make Hanukah so special this year if I got Pearl and I could transform her into the rich Pearl!"

My mother's answer did not please me at all! "I think that doll is a ridiculous idea and offensive. Why would they promote such a doll all over the TV. I don't know what you like about her but I am not going to be a part of getting this doll for you... so don't expect to see her anytime soon. You will get a doll... more than likely but one that is more wholesome than Pearl."

Wow... such a strong reaction from my Mom! I guess I better just forget about Pearl after all... but it's so hard to do so as every day I see her on TV and I liked the transformation so much! Well, I hope the doll I do get will be good... but I am sure not as good as Pearl!

So Hanukah arrived and on the first night I got a baby doll with a layette. I did like this doll a lot and especially appreciated that she came with a full wardrobe and baby bottle for me to really act like her mother. I immediately began spending hours of time imagining with my new baby. It made me almost forget about Pearl who was still appearing on TV as an advertisement for Christmas... almost forget... but not completely.

We got a gift every night for the eight nights. Most nights were small presents from aunts or my grandmother. Generally, after the first night it was all downhill... most of the other gifts were not so exciting.

But then one night a "new big gift" appeared on the table by the menorah for me! I did not expect another big gift...what could it be... and who could have gotten it for me?

After the blessings were said over the candles and the lights were glowing... I ripped open my gift and there was Pearl... looking of course at that moment Pitiful! Oh my God I exclaimed... I got her after all!

And who was she from? My brother Martin.

He had sat by listening to my entreaty for the doll... and my mother's answer about why she was a ridiculous doll to buy... and he tucked it all away... and made his own plan to surprise me with Pearl.

He quietly went about finding her in the toy store and having her wrapped and hid her away at home until the right moment.

I threw my arms around his neck and told him how much I loved him!

This was my brother...

OK so he defied my mother's wishes on this one just to please his little sister... but somehow that was important to him... finding the way to my heart.

And after all was said and done my mother overlooked this small act of defiance and admitted she was pleased that he had so very much pleased me.

Martin and Poor Pitiful Pearl had enriched my Hanukah immensely. Hanukah was transformed... and then I quickly went about transforming Pearl... into rich Pearl... and I introduced her to the baby I had gotten from my mother.

Mother was right of course... it was a crazy concept. Once she had been transformed to "rich Pearl" I did not see the sense of sending her back to her former self... that would have been quite pitiful!

The privilege of summer camp

WE WERE A very ordinary middle class family that had aspirations of a higher social standing. My mother was always the one who knew to reach higher and pushed to do so. It meant that we dressed like we had more money than we actually had...we entertained like we had more money than we actually had... and summer camp was just one more place that we emulated those who actually could afford to go to overnight camp.

Martin was the first of us to go to sleep away camp and for him mother chose a fancier camp than when Jo Ann and I would go in later years. Martin went to Camp Log N'Twig in the Poconos. Pocono camps were thought to be the "better" camps.

Summer Camp...what were we all to do and learn there?

Summer Camp... an idyllic getaway from city life.

Cooler breezes up in the Poconos when summer in the city can be oppressive.

Friends to live with and embrace for lifelong friendships.

Developing independence and autonomy.

Swimming and boating and fishing in the lake.

Proficiency in swimming, baseball, tennis, archery, riflery, basketball, etc.

Learning about nature in a natural setting.

A wholesome sense of community.

It sounds like I am writing the voiceover for a commercial for sleep-away camp. All of these things led my mother--ultimately my parents-- to decide to send Martin to Camp Log N' Twig. In this idyllic surrounding Martin would find himself and learn to become proficient in athletics and finally develop real friendships that would last a lifetime.

Guess what? Camp was not going to be the answer for Martin either. The summer that Martin was at that camp there were serious storms that impacted the Poconos. There were days when we had no idea at all whether he and his camp mates were safe from flood waters. When communication was finally resumed, we found out that the floods at camp had finally provided Martin something to excel in. Where the other campers felt penned in and antsy because they could not take part in the regular camp activities; Martin reveled in all that the hurricane had wrought.

This was right up his alley. He convinced the leadership at the camp that they needed to use the row-boats to travel around the camp bunk to bunk... and find out what each bunk needed to pass the hours confined to quarters. He was so excited about this prospect that they allowed Martin to go out each day with them in the boat... enter the bunks and take down the requests. Later in the day, he again returned with the booty that was requested. He loved that flood. It won him notice and notoriety at Camp Log N'Twig... he was like the Mayor... visiting his people in a time of disaster and trying to make the difficulty less troubling. He never tired of those visits... and he came to know all of the campers this way. He was disappointed when the waters dissipated and normality resumed.

For him... that was the tragedy... now he would have to resume all of the camp activities that he deplored.

Boating for him was not on the lake... it was boating around the flooded campgrounds... feeling important and popular.

Who wanted to play ball or go on a hike? He hated all of these activities.

And the friendships? Those did not really materialize either... he enjoyed being known... that was as far as he ever wanted to go with friendship.

But at camp, he did show his autonomy and his ingenuity with his plan to visit the bunks by boat. That was the kind of camper he was. When there was trouble and disaster at camp he was at his best... his happiest. He could solve a problem like no one else... his mind always going in this way.

He went to that camp only that one summer. We have pictures of him there with my parents on visiting day... all of them looking pleased that he was there. But...they sent him there to be like all of the other "guys" and he took advantage of none of the normal activities... no need to splurge on this extravagance again.

"You know Martin...we are always trying to get him to be like everyone else... and he never conforms. He takes every activity that we have chosen for him... and invents something that we had not considered... better save money than squander it on such frivolity!"

We had arrived!!

IT WAS 1960 and the Hess family was moving into a new home... one we would own, after spending the last seven years in a rented rowhouse. My mother detested that house and everything about living in the "less good" neighborhood.

And so we arrived...

1119 E. Barringer Street represented a major step up for our family. The house was "semi-detached"... and had three bedrooms and two full bathrooms and two half bathrooms. It had a recreation room instead of a basement... it had a lawn and a front and side patio. All of us loved this house.

The neighborhood was almost 100 percent Jewish and I bet that every Jewish family there was attempting to follow a similar script. The neighborhood represented "suburbia" within the confines of Philadelphia. It was here that families in the summer had patio furniture and barbecues... and perhaps even an above ground swimming pool. Most families had a car parked in front of the house and another one in the drive-way.

My mother had help with decorating this house. The house was replete with new draperies and new wall-paper in every room. In the living room the wall over the sofa was adorned by a "roman mural"... which we thought was elegant and now I realize was hideous. There were wall-to-wall carpets in every room. The new living room furniture was a white brocade long sofa and upholstered chairs and loveseat. When I met my husband years later... also living in this neighborhood the furnishings in his house... the cars in the front of the house and in the drive... were almost identical.

We were all striving upwards... and our homes represented the fulfillment of the dream... part one.

Part two related to the dreams for the children in these striving Jewish families. We were to be top-notch students in the Philadelphia public schools that we attended. We were to look forward to college... for the boys so that they could pursue a profession... for the girls so that they could meet a husband... who was a professional.

After school the children attended Hebrew school... mainly in this neighborhood... but for my family we continued with the synagogue we had always attended in East Oak Lane.

In the Summer... if the family was able there would be summer camp. At first this might just be day camp... but for those families that had "really arrived" it was sleep away camp... and possibly that was for the entire eight weeks of summer. There were also forays to Atlantic City... for a part or all of the summer.

For me... it was not said in so many words... but I understood that I was to reach higher than this for my life as an adult. I was to marry a man who would be richer... than my parents. I was to arrange my life so that I had a finer home... and cars... and vacations... than my parents had... and hopefully would not develop any money problems to create this life. I was to want only this... nothing more for myself and the next generation. I imbibed this script... this formula and was able to follow parts of it... as did my sister and most of the women in our middle-class neighborhood and socio-economic grouping.

It took not so many years of marriage and the feminist movement to have me striving for much more in my life and for much more for my own children.

But my brother... he just was not able to fit the mold of the East Mt. Airy Jewish family of the 1960's...

He disdained everything about this existence.

He told me so:

One night I sat with him in his small and cozy bedroom and he and I were discussing life and our aspirations in life. I was around fifteen and that he was almost twenty two. One of the issues that we were unpacking was the fact that he had been dating a non-Jewish girl and that my parents had found out. He told me that night that my father warned him that if he continued to date a "shiksa" he would "sit shiva" for him and disown him. In very traditional Jewish homes this would be the approach if a child married out of the faith... it was considered to be a "shandah" (a shame to the family). I asked Martin what he was going to do about it...would he stop seeing her so to avoid this family cut-off? I was terrified that this would actually come to be and that I would lose my brother.

He had a simple story that he told me then. He explained to me that the life that our family was living was simple and boring and that it did not interest him. He asked me: "Do you want to be like mother and daddy ... going to work every day and working too hard... and always having money problems?" I must have told him... that I hoped to have more money someday... but actually the life we had was one I hoped for. (although I did profess to want to be a doctor... even then... but was not fully cognizant of how much serious study this would entail).

Well, Martin let me know that night that this life was not for him and that he would not be dictated to about how he would live his adult life. When I asked him what this really meant... he quite simply told me that he aspired to make a lot of money... he did not care how he did it. He knew he would never go to work every day... like my parents did... and still have a sense that he was not rich! He would be rich one way or the other. I had no idea what he could have meant by this... .how would you get this money Martin? He could not yet put that into words for me... but he knew that he would find "an angle" to do so. As for the non-Jewish girlfriend... who he professed to love... he said he would be with her and if the parents had to "sit shiva" so be it. (Ironically, when shiva was to be observed after his death... it never happened... my parents could not face anyone... there was too much shame,) I recently learned from my sister that Martin had possibly fathered a child with this woman... one that none of us had ever seen... that child would have been my parent's first grandchild . (all of my research has let me know that even then Martin had begun his relationships with many of the unsavory characters that would be his undoing.)

I left his room feeling that he had confided in me... and that I was disturbed by all that he said... even though I didn't understand it... or believe him. I suppose I hoped that "this too shall pass."

As Jo Ann and I fulfilled the destiny that we were meant for... Martin must have looked on us with dismay... laughing inside that we could not see how stereotypical our lives had become.

Yes... we both followed the script... but I believe that Martin's problems... and ultimately his death... caused both of his sisters... to reach outside the limited messages that had been delivered to each of us and reinvent ourselves.

I was to dream beyond my parents expectations. If only Martin could have lived to see what we were to become. I imagine a great deal of it would have shocked him.

The family celebrates Christmas at the Golden Slipper Supper Club

Besefer Hayim: In the book of life, blessing, and peace, and proper sustenance may we be remembered and inscribed for a good life and for peace

AT THE BEGINNING of the Jewish New Year on Rosh Hashanah we intone these words repeatedly... and they have always had the power to catch in my throat the first time that I chant them, knowing all that I hope for all those in my life that I love... a group that has expanded with the years of my life and with increasing knowledge of all that can go well and can go awry in the course of one year. We enter the synagogue each year... look around and can see who has had a difficult inscription from the year just ending.

So it seemed this particular year of my memory... began with much potential for good... I will take you back to it with me. I was a teenager in the Rosh Hashanah that I am uncovering and we all still lived in the house on Barringer Street. At this time, my brother was juggling a new set of jobs that kept him going at all times. He still worked with my parents at the family store... but he also had several other jobs. His main "other" means of employment was in running movie theaters(both indoor theaters and drive-in movie theaters) for a major developer of these venues, Claude Schlanger. He met Mr. Schlanger when he was working with Hy Lit. The connection between these two revolved around the venues... as some of Hy Lit's shows were held at Mr. Schlanger's theaters or drive-ins. Both Claude and Hy Lit were taken with my brother and his creative initiative. He was able to really bring good energy to both endeavors and they both found increasing ways to make use of his talents.

So what does all of this have to do with Rosh Hashanah? It was our family custom to have an extensive open house for Rosh Hashanah for family and friends... and it seemed to grow exponentially every year. The year that Martin was working for both of these men he asked them to come to the family open house... as he wanted to introduce them to his parents and for them to know his roots. Mr. Schlanger was not Jewish... Hy Lit was. Martin was proud of his family and he was proud of these two "big shots"... both prominent enough to be known in the wider world... and he wanted my parents and all of us to know his connection... and his value to them.

Martin was quite excited about the guests that he had included for the open house this year... and the rest of us were too. It seemed so clear that including them might mean that this was opening a time of "sustenance and blessing" for him. If these prominent figures believed in him to such a degree ... it seemed that he was finally on his way to his pathway in life. Martin was someone that this man could rely on to run a part of his business with competence. If he could just stick with Mr. Schlanger there was no telling what the future could mean for him.

My mother always took the days before the holidays off from the store to cook and bake for this open house. She baked her Apple cake, cinnamon bow ties, butter horns, and chocolate and jelly pastry squares every year. She also made pickled herring and several kugels. We were not kosher in our home so we were fine mixing the dairy pastries with brisket sandwiches and sweet and sour meatballs. My mother set a table laden with all of her artistry. This was her favorite time ... when she could be at home creating I sat with Martin in synagogue as we waited to go home.. Martin began to quiz me about the food that I knew mother had prepared, as I was often allowed to help her in these preparations. I rattled off the list to him... and I could see that he seemed troubled. "Martin, what is wrong with the items for the lunch buffet it is what mother always makes," I reminded him. He let me know that now he found this list too skimpy, he was worried that the table might not be full to overflowing and sufficiently impress his guests. What were we to do, I asked him as it was already the holiday... and the lunch was scheduled in just hours back at the house. He said: "We have to get out of here and go marketing... right now!" It did not seem to me the right thing to do as we were supposed to be praying to be inscribed for a good year ahead, but off I went with him to make sure that there would be only happiness and hospitality on display when all of the guests arrived.

We left the synagogue and were off to the Penn Fruit market on Ogontz Ave, not far away from our synagogue. We bought the place out, more herring, white fish, lox and bagels, and packaged cakes. Most of this food was out of place on my mother's usual Rosh Hashanah lunch table, but the motivation was quantity, not my mother's quality. Martin was adamant that we could not be seen as having a skimpy lunch and so many guests. After we bought all of this bounty we went straight home and arranged the table with both my mother's delicacies and all of our purchases. My parents were a bit shocked when they arrived home from synagogue to see everything already set-up... and my mother was shocked by all that we had added to her menu. But the motivation was immediately understood and was not seen as problematic... and now we awaited the special guests... and all of our usual family and friends. I was most excited that Martin expected Hy Lit to come to our house. This was really a big deal for a teenager in the time of Bandstand. I would have much to tell my friends.

Mr. Schlanger and his wife did come to the lunch... Hy Lit never showed. But my parents were quite pleased to meet Claude and treated him like royalty. My brother was the main event of the open house with everyone happy to meet his successful entrepreneurial boss. Claude had many laudatory things to share with my parents about Martin and they and Martin seemed to be bursting with pride. The spread of food was commented on by everyone, how copious it was and how delicious the array.

The first day of Rosh Hashanah that year ended on such a high note. It seemed that finally Martin had found the way in his life to be inscribed for all good. He had found his calling managing the "work of others." And he was good at it. My parents heard from Claude that he had so much more potential than they had ever ascribed to about him. Their prayers... so heartfelt were being answered. They looked at their son that day and saw a pathway forward for him... one that he had worked hard to develop on his own. They were sure from the words of this important man that Martin would also be important someday.

And in the book of life and blessing may you be inscribed...

Martin seemed to have taken these words in in the past year... and was finding his way to life and blessing... for this... we all prayed.

We pray on Rosh Hashanah for sustenance . Martin needed his sustenance to be colored always with drama and excitement, and then it would not be able to last... it would always blow up at some point along the way.

We would pray these words yearly, and this particular year it seemed to feel possible.

Yom Kippur

IT IS YOM Kippur... the most solemn day of the Jewish year. Even on such a day... my brother was able to make the entire experience an adventure. The adventure for him often began immediately as we arrived at the synagogue on Kol Nidre eve. Yom Kippur requires a Jew to undertake a fast for 25 hours. So an appropriate meal was enjoyed at home before we took off for shul... and in spite of this my brother was already rustling the troops when he arrived at Emanu-El to accompany him to the Hot Shoppe for cheeseburgers (a no no on any day... but especially not on Yom Kippur!!!).

I was six years his junior and so this particular escapade was not one I would be a part of as I was not the demographic he was rustling up.... and I am sure the proper, well behaved child that I was... would not allow me to join in at all. But the synagogue was just one of those places that my brother saw as a place to push the envelope... and get others to go along with him. For me, the synagogue was a place of magic and mystery... both of which Martin had helped to spin for me.

What he did inveigle me into with him... was sneaking into the main sanctuary for the service... without the required ticket. Our synagogue was a very "high church" place of worship. It seemed massive and imposing... with marble and gold and a balcony. In its time the High Holidays had multiple services going on simultaneously... and the main service was, of course, the place to be. Seats were assigned and costly... the front row seats of course for the very wealthy "machers" (big shots). My family were not machers! My parents did have seats in the main service with their closest friends... but the children were not so lucky... unless very rich!!!

So I was always gullible with my brother and his schemes-- he knew just how to invite me in. Somehow he knew how to "fast talk" the ushers and he and I would waltz in to the empty seats on row five... right in front of the watchful eyes of Rabbi Maxwell M. Farber... and that was the way we referred to him... even the initial was crucial. He was the king of the bimah. He was imposing, bombastic and a bit scary. He was a rabbi who banged on the pulpit to make a point... and he was a rabbi that required 100 percent decorum. As I joined my brother in this pursuit... I would ask him innocently if we were going to pray from the prayer books at the seats we were sneaking into this time. Martin would always assure me that that was the purpose of our entering... this holy place... to fully partake in prayer. He had found the way for us (he and I) to partake of and witness the splendor in this main palace of Judaism.

It would not take very long until his idea of prayer and mine diverged. I had the book open and was trying to follow... and he would be issuing commentary not only on the actions of the rabbi... but also on the lady in front of us who he deemed ridiculous for one reason or another(the hat, the clothes, the perfume). It really did not matter, he would find something to make a joke about. Within the first ten minutes he would reduce me to uncontrollable laughter... and we would get that all knowing look from Rabbi Maxwell M. Farber... and an obvious request for us to leave the seats not rightfully ours to begin with. By the time we were again in the foyer... I would be ashamed and furious with him for conning me into this act... on Yom Kippur... yet! But I was with him... and at his side... and I could see the obvious joy in his face that he had brought me into his adventure... and had caused me to both laugh and feel the shame. That was my brother...... it is illustrative of a pattern that repeated through many episodes in our lives together.

The family travelled together to synagogue in our car, with my father driving. But once the Yom Kippur holiday set in he would not ride. So Mother drove home from synagogue alone and we accompanied Daddy on the trip home. We did not live close to the synagogue so it was at least an hour walk each way. We walked through East Oak Lane Philadelphia to East Mt. Airy. It was always dark on the way home.

The walk home often had my father teaching us, what were the messages that we were to be taking this year from Yom Kippur? He explained that it was the holiday in which we needed to ask for forgiveness from God for all that we had done wrong in the year that had passed. He emphasized to us that now was the time to begin again, fresh in an effort to be our best selves. That is what the shofar is calling you to do... my father would emphasize. This was a treasured time with my father. He was generally at his best on this walk... my father the "religious expert of the family." I loved hearing him hold forth about the meaning of this time, I took it all in and I took it to heart. He would also invariably share stories of his growing up in the shetetl in Austria/Poland and what he had learned from his own father about the holiday.

Jo Ann and I tagged along perhaps reviewing the latest fashions that we had observed in our peers or the women's outfits that were totally up- to-date... Daddy and Martin were in the front of us... Daddy lecturing Martin. Jo Ann and I heard the same talk from behind every year "Martin, I hope you were listening to the rabbi tonight. He encouraged each of us to evaluate our misdeeds from the past year and vow to do a better job this year. I don't really want to list all of the things you did wrong last year but you and I know well that there is much to improve upon. You could begin by paying more attention in school and worrying less about how to make a buck. Every year, that lecture would be even longer if Daddy knew all that Jo Ann and I knew about what Martin even did during Yom Kippur. Martin would organize the others who were willing to go with him to the Hot Shoppe on Broad Street for cheeseburgers and floats. Martin would also think up other high jinx in the mysterious building ... seemingly mammoth to me as a child... that were inviting to many of the teens that he attracted. He was like the Pied Piper of Congregation Emanu-el. He knew parts of the synagogue building that seemed to be secret to everyone else. He took all of us on scavenger hunts to every nook and cranny that held the secrets of this building. Sometimes it was just to escape the building and join all of the other teens out on the steps of that awesome building. The steps became the place that all of the important developments of the year that had passed would be shared with peers. Martin did allow me to stand with him on the steps... at times. When he did he gave me the confidence to show that I was "cool" too.

If my father were to find out about all of these "misdeeds" it would begin the New Year with screaming and disappointment immediately. My brother was a Jew...one who questioned and argued about what made sense to him in his Judaism... and what did not. He was never able to convince my father of the rightness of his acts... not on Kol Nidre night...probably not at all. While we walked miles together to get home on Kol Nidre night the distance would never be long enough for my father and my brother to reach a place of agreement. As we lived miles from our synagogue, they, Daddy and Martin "lived" miles apart in life, perpetually.

What my father could not recognize as positive about Martin and his Yom Kippur activities was actually seen ultimately as positive from the leadership of our synagogue. Martin had been quite active in United Synagogue Youth, in fact he was the President of his chapter. He had gotten other teens to be excited about joining the chapter and once he was out of High School one of his first paid positions was to be the Youth Director of our synagogue. Just as he invited other young people to take part in his Yom Kippur adventures, he was able to attract many teens to join a chapter that had not always been so popular. I know my parents were pleased by this development, if not a bit surprised. Their son, the one who seemed incorrigible at times, now had his own office in our family synagogue. For a while, this too became a source of pride for both my mother and father, and I must admit, for me too.

Martin quickly transformed this chapter into an active and bustling one with activities that pleased all of the teens that were members. This all began well. There would be record hops in the synagogue that were attended by members of the chapters and perhaps members of another chapter. This was what was expected. After some time, these mundane record hops began to bore Martin. While he was working with the teens at the synagogue, he was also working with the popular disc jockey Hy Lit. Martin claimed to be his "manager." So, in usual Martin fashion, he began to imagine that his work at the synagogue and his work with Hy Lit could be merged into something that would bring more synergy to his endeavors. The next record Hop he arranged for Hy Lit to appear at the synagogue. He advertised it widely and droves of teens showed up at the synagogue for this event. The first few times that this happened it was all accepted by the synagogue leadership. They appreciated that the chapter was raising unbelievable sums of money! At some point it was obvious that these events were no longer "Jewish teen" events but city-wide rock music venues. When that became crystal clear they brought Martin in and asked him to leave his job as Youth Director. They told him that he had developed something on his own without the proper authorization. They did not want to be a venue for his "other activities." Martin, they told him, "You do not seem to understand the goals or the scope of USY!"

After his dismissal, that Yom Kippur walk home was done in greater silence. My father began to understand that his lectures were not getting through to his son. While Martin seemed to like the synagogue and being attached to it, he did not like it enough to keep it safe from his other pursuits. My father took this in and seethed with anger at this son of his, whom he clearly saw this son as nothing but trouble.

How had we embraced this myth?

THE MYTH: "A nice Jewish Boy does not get into trouble with the law!"

The family: My family believed this and believed that we were the first family to ever have a family member involved with organized crime, and our belief did not allow us to discuss this fact with anyone.

In her book, *Masculinity and the Making of American Judaism,* Sarah Imhoff discusses Jewish men who found their way to criminal behavior. It seems my brother's experience had not been so unique after all.

From this book, I learned:

- New York Police Commissioner Bingham wrote in 1908: "There was a gentle art of Jewish crime and a lack of aggressiveness and courage of Jewish criminals which stood in sharp contrast to the audacity and courage of Italian criminals." (Imhoff pg. 209)
- Jewish leaders countered Bingham's article by positing that: "Judaism would help form young Jews who would grow up to be upstanding members of the community instead of criminals, and second, communal leaders would unite New York Jewry under the banner of Judaism." (Imhoff, pg. 216)
- A rabbi spoke about crime in his Yom Kippur sermon and felt that the synagogue would be the cure for any attraction to a life of crime. Judaism, he believed was a cure for the possibility of crime.
- Jews believed that if there was a Jewish man who was truly a gangster, he was the exception, and could not have been reached through connection

to the community or the synagogue. This then was not a "Jewish" problem, it was an anomaly. And the community response to the outlier was silence and no recognition.

- In a later chapter Imhoff offers this generalization about Jewish male criminals based upon her study of materials connected to the crime committed by Leo Frank who was accused of a murder of a factory worker, Mary Phagan in 1913: "Jews do not get into bar brawls. They do not beat their wives. Jewish men are not physically aggressive or violent. Jews might embezzle money or commit fraud, but not assault and certainly not murder. These images suggest the borders of Jewish masculinity." (Imhoff, page 238)
- When Jewish men did commit crimes it was assumed both by Jews and non-Jews they were of a certain sort: perhaps conniving or profit-driven, but without violence, confrontation, or aggression. Jewish crimes, then, were not manly crimes. Those Jewish crimes that took on another nature and were violent were often explained as due to abnormal sexuality; those men were seen as perverts. (Imhoff, page 266)

Imhoff's book was not the first book I had ingested on this topic. Years earlier while a rabbinical student I read extensively about this phenomena for a paper I was writing for a course. In my reading so much of what I read about Bugsy Siegal or Myer Lansky had overtones of our experiences. One book in particular was quite valuable for my understanding. *Tough Jews, Fathers and Sons and Gangster Dreams* by Rich Cohen. The title in particular resonated for me—Gangster Dreams. Perhaps it was the glamour and the fantasy that first attracted my brother to that fatal route.

Cohen suggested in his understanding of the Jewish gangster story that perhaps it was the "Jewish story" of oppression throughout the ages that invited some into the life of crime. Smuggling drugs in particular, he felt offered a way to believe things could have happened in a different way. The drugs, acting as antidote, for years of slavery, living as guests in the land of others, and destruction. (Tough Jews, pg. 132)

He also offered that in families, the choices made amongst siblings can be diametrically opposed. In his words: "one brother goes into hardware, the other into opium." (TJ, pg. 139). I read these words and it shines a light onto my own life and my confusion. How come I was able to be so "good" and conventional while Martin had to go so far astray? Oh, the Hess family had not invented this scenario after all.

Cohen attested to the fact that some of the men who took the route of crime were in fact brilliant. Their flaw was often restlessness and a drive that lit their minds from within. The drive was connected to their desire to rise above, to never chance tasting poverty—they were first and foremost ambitious. The ambition often misguided. They could have chosen Wall Street but they chose just any street. The skills needed in both places were quite similar. On one street there were some legal constraints; on the other there were none. The motivation developed from a similar "Jewish narrative."

Cohen's research also provided insight that our family lacked, and that my brother the "dreamer" could not have understood as he entered this world.

Cohen states, "They joined the Mob when they were young, before they knew what it was about. Only later, after the first robbery, the first killing, did the picture come into focus. This is a world where no one is trusted, where no one walks away, a world without windows or doors. And by then it was too late.

"Now and then, someone did try to get out. He would go all around the candy store, shaking hands. He had fallen in love or found God or whatever. He had forgotten something too... that the last person who had fallen in love or found God or whatever had turned up in the weeds." (TJ, pg. 145)

When my parents advised my brother to be a Mensch—to walk away and to talk about others that he had been involved with in the drug smuggling deal, they did not know the rules of the game that he had gotten into. He might have, but he followed the "Jewish script" instead and wound up dead.

I discovered that we were not the first Jewish family to produce a gangster, a teacher/principal, and a rabbi.

Way back in 1897, Louis(Lepke) Buchalter was born on the Lower East Side in Manhattan. In his storied career as a mobster he was also the brother of a rabbi, a dentist and a teacher. (Rockaway, pg. 24). Children could clearly grow up in the same Jewish home, celebrate the same holidays and get similar messages and then choose to travel to such different places in life.

The wayward and defiant son: Deuteronomy 21:18-21

MY EYE CATCHES on that one section, Deuteronomy 21:18-21: "This son of ours is wayward and defiant, he does not heed us, he is a glutton and a drunkard. The men of our town shall stone him to death."

Quite extreme: he will be stoned to death! In my study of this section I learn that the rabbis were so concerned about this injunction being carried out that they made it impossible for parents to do so. The rabbis set up conditions that they were quite sure would never come to pass. Nothing untoward would happen to this wayward son if both parents were not in total agreement. The rabbis were certain that it would never happen that both parents would believe that their own flesh and blood were so defiant that death should be the answer.

The biblical text makes it so clear that what I had thought was only happening in the Hess family...was an age-old problem. Parents had always had children that they could not control, or who remained a mystery to them. In the biblical text, sadly, we learn that to go public with this challenge was to admit failure and thus risk that others would take the matter into their hands, on your behalf.

The text rang in my ears... it matched so closely with the research and writing that had been with me for years... about my brother and his "wayward" acts.

The rabbis fully understood my parents and the internal family battle that such a wayward child presented to parents. In their effort to assure that a parent would never bring their son to the elders of the town for stoning... they developed a "law"... a halakah in Talmud that stated:

"If the father wants to have him punished but not the mother, or if the father does not want him punished but the mother does, he is not considered wayward and defiant. Both parents must see the situation eye to eye." (BT Sandhedrin 8:4)

Wow the rabbis got my family! It was a common occurrence that Martin would do the defiant thing, my father would "want to kill him for it" and my mother would want to embrace him tighter, to show Martin he was loved and valued. This dance was eternal, and so fortunately Martin was not brought to the elders of the town to be stoned to death.

That is, until the very end.

When he sat in jail and faced real punishment my parents both convinced him that it was the time to come to the elders (the US government that is) and fully cooperate with them in order to escape punishment and obtain a chance to start over.

The elders, they took that information from him and failed to protect him once they possessed it.

Word got out, and he was "stoned to death" by other men of the town.

When my mother and father finally saw "eye to eye" about their "wayward" son and shared that with him, his fate was sealed.

"He does not heed us... the men of the town shall stone him to death."

If only mother had held out.

PART III

The Other Side of the Underworld

Officer Marty

Jo Ann

"He found something he wanted, had always wanted and always would want—not to be admired, as he had feared; not to be loved, as he made himself believe; but to be necessary to people, to be indispensable."
—F. Scott Fitzgerald, This Side of Paradise

FREDI WRITES, "I *always knew that day would come." I did not. My life was filled with the mundane activities of raising a family. I can honestly say that I didn't give our brother's problems much thought. He had gotten himself involved in organized crime with his eyes wide open. He never believed there would be horrifying consequences for his actions. The result would lead to a reality that left all of us reeling in our own private desperation.*

The issues were always with what happened when his creations became successful and moderately lucrative. Our parents supported his idea to expand the linen store into the custom drapery business. Neither my mother nor father knew anything about measuring or handing or selling custom drapes. They fully believed that Martin's business acumen would be the answer to improving their lot in the retail business. Initially it was. But... then, like every other endeavor, Martin grew bored with only two plates spinning. He had to branch out to other venues: merchandising marts in Montgomeryville, PA and New Jersey. This was another instance of failure in the end. He would prove himself and his aspirations which were funded by his parents initially; but, later on were the result of his convincing others to invest in his schemes.

I believe he thought he could "always get away with it" whatever the "it" would be because his whole life was a reflection of that belief. At a shiva for an uncle, Martin grew bored. All of the children were asked to go outside to Woodbury Avenue, Wynnefield when all of the cousins were together. Once again, he had to draw negative attention to himself by finding and placing a cat in one of the cars. Most would view this behavior as merely "mischievous," but for him, it was the driving force, modus operandi. He knew it was wrong and that he would be punished but he did it anyway. This resulting in the ongoing question "why?"

There are no easy answers to understanding his motivation. He was well aware he was "special and favorite" for his mother; and constantly confrontational with his father. Some of his efforts were intentional: to prove he could produce better earnings and outcomes than his father. Did he intuit his father's dissatisfaction with his personal station in life? Was it necessary to constantly put this in his face by embarrassing, failing and going to extremes to gain attention? Did negative response give Martin greater satisfaction than positive gains? This was the mystery of his life and his lifestyle.

I never had the opportunity to confront Martin in the midst of his demise. Although, I was aware he was in trouble, I had no idea how deeply involved he had become with the mafia. Initially, he would describe the people interacting with him at this juncture as "exciting and successful." These were people who convinced him that he could be part of a rapid ride to enormous and easy wealth. As this was always enticing to him, no risk was ever too great if it resulted in riches. No different from his younger escapades, he believed that no trip to Jamaica or to Afghanistan was too dangerous... he always returned with greater wealth.

What happened to Martin would not garner headlines in today's press. It would just be another footnote in the current culture of bad deeds. But 45 years ago, it was a hot story with so many mafia overtones the public found enticing. To our family it was a Shonda... a disgrace that brought shame and anger to everyone.

Fredi: Martin thought he could waltz into the underworld and just fit in

PHILADELPHIA IN THE 60's and early 70's was a center of the underworld in our country... it involved a smaller crime family than in other cities but it was strategically positioned within Cosa Nostra. The Boss of the Philadelphia family was a member of the Mafia Commission. Philadelphia's status as a mob city was only enhanced by the fact that its orbit also extended to New Jersey and especially to Atlantic City.

In a book about the Philadelphia mob, by George Anastasia entitled Blood and Honor he described the atmosphere in South Philadelphia, the seat of the crime family:

"Nurtured by family ties and Old World values, residents of South Philadelphia have given the city a long list of prominent doctors, lawyers, judges and athletes who have had a positive impact on the community. Their contributions outweigh the impact of crime and corruption generated by the neighborhood's one nefarious institution. But there is no denying that South Philadelphia has stocked three generations supplying a core group of thieves, loan sharks, extortionists, and murderers who have corrupted and bastardized those same family ties and values." (pg. 32)

So in South Philadelphia there was also two disparate pathways open to a man of that time to follow. One respected by most in the neighborhood... the other respected and revered by those who were part of the "family."

In describing one of the mobsters, Anastasia said of him "he was a born hustler and natural con man. And the mob was the only institution that put any stock in those talents. It was seen as a distortion of the values of that mobster's true community. It was by his own admission... the dark side of the Italian American work ethic."

Change "Italian" to "Jewish" and Anastasia could have been describing my brother:

"The courtship began on the corner at Seventh and Morris where Caramandi, a fifteen year old high school dropout, hung out with a group of older teenagers. Their talk was of drugs and money and girls. Their heroes were the guys from the neighborhood with connections and juice... the bookmakers, gamblers, and loan sharks who worked with or for the Angelo Bruno organization. Caramandi listened and learned." (pg. 33)

Later he paints a picture of Caramandi's style

"When he had money in his pocket he dressed the part of a South Philadelphia wiseguy in a tailored suit and silk tie, or a cashmere sports jacket and Italian leather loafers. Short and stocky with thick black hair and an engaging roguish style, Caramandi was playing the role of a mobster long before he became one. Money was always first on his list." (pg. 35)

He could have been outlining my brother's evolution into a life of a criminal. The big difference was Martin was a transplant to South Philadelphia. He had not grown up in this culture drinking in its rules and its mores.

He literally came from the other end of town, almost like suburbia in comparison to South Philadelphia. And the values were not the old world Italian values, he was raised with Judaism, present in the very air we breathed.

And in the Jewish neighborhood that he was living in the currency was "striving." The striving took the form of seeking an education that would allow anyone who availed himself/herself the chance to reach above the level of the parents. Where the parents were often merchants, they hoped to see their children become doctors and lawyers.

Like Caramandi, Martin could not see himself as someone who could succeed in this fashion. He too was born a hustler; it was in his blood. Reaching back even into his childhood, Martin was on the street learning how to make a dime in any way possible. He sold my mother's sweaters right out of her drawer and then used that money to buy her a "present," not really comprehending that his gift was corrupted by her loss of sweaters.

In this Jewish, striving culture, he never was able to fit in. He looked different from his peers and sought out the guys that looked and acted tough.

Ultimately the lure of South Philadelphia would be real for him. He found himself there and he could see men who appealed to his view of his talents. But he had not been raised to understand the makeup of the mob or mobsters. He had been raised "to be a good Jewish boy."

So, like Caramandi he began to dress the part first to look like he fit in. In the atmosphere of South Philadelphia he learned some of how to bring his own street talents to the men that worked this beat for their entire lives. He tried to be one of them, and eventually got "in" with the real players.

But no one just waltzes into this world lacking years of insight and gets out of it alive.

To us he was Martin, to them he was Marty

APRIL 1969.

I read in an article about the very involved scheme that my brother was involved in that his involvement with some of the main players in his death began way before our family ever could have imagined.

The article entitled "Philadelphia Connection: Intrigue on Three Continents" introduced the relationship that my brother had with Police Lieutenant Joseph Marker. According to this article, by April 1969 they had known each other for over eight years. That would mean that when my brother was living with all of us in our lovely home at 1119 Barringer Street, he was already learning about the narcotics trade in Philadelphia from some of the professionals.

Customs officials knew all about my brother and his activities. They stated that calls were made from my brother's business phone to Lt. Marker repeatedly in April and May of 1969. It also recorded that some of the calls that Martin made about the "deal" were actually made from Marker's home.

Marker testified that he had lost touch with Martin after this and then did not hear from him again until May of 1971, when Martin reported to him that "a big thing was coming very soon."

The big thing happened over three continents... It began in London... then on to Greece and Turkey... from there Afghanistan... on to India and Mombasa Kenya... and finally back to the USA in New York...

I don't even know how the brother that grew up at my side could have known about all of those places and continents. We knew about Philadelphia,

Atlantic City, New York... and in April of 1969 Bermuda... as I was planning my honeymoon... that was it... 100 percent!

I spent a fair amount of time with Martin in those same months. It was of course the "other Martin"... my big brother.

It was just months before my wedding so that was a major topic of conversation in the family. Our lovely home at 1119 Barringer Street was up for sale.

My parents were willing to sell the house and move into an apartment so that their little daughter, who was marrying the handsome medical student, could have a wedding with "all the trimmings" just like in the movie "Goodbye Columbus." I fulfilled my parents' desire and married a professional.

I did not want to cause my parents financial pressure... I was "willing" to have a lesser wedding... but they would have none of it. The wedding would be as beautiful as my sister's wedding had been!

I told Martin all of my fears about this. "Martin, I am so worried that because of me and this fancy wedding our parents will have serious financial difficulties." He would listen and then he would dispel my angst... "just go ahead and enjoy every minute of it" he would advise. He never told me that he resented my sister and I for all of the "goodies" that were rained down on us the two "appropriate" Jewish children. He acted only as my counselor, but I believe that in his soul he was seething with anger for all that Jo Ann and I got for so little effort.

The house was sold in time to pay for the bash, the sale almost fell through at the last minute, but it happened and the bills were able to be paid. There was enough money to pay for the band, the elaborate flowers, the abundant hors d'oeuvres and the upgraded Prime Rib dinner.

Martin meanwhile... in the midst of all of his scheming was carpeting my parents new apartment and then the apartment I would move into after the wedding. This was "his gift" both to the parents and to the bridal couple.

And Martin and I planned a sweet surprise for my parents at the wedding. The week of the wedding would also be their thirtieth wedding anniversary—and Martin's 28th birthday. So the two of us contacted the orchestra leader and the caterer asking for anniversary cake and a special dance in their honor. It all came off without a hitch at the wedding and there is a picture in my wedding album of the special cake and my mother showing her surprise that her two children, Martin and Fredi had assured that this was a part of the celebration.

So there you have it…

While one version of my brother was working on the grand scheme with criminals for an involved narcotics ring…

The other version was just in our lives as son and brother in all of the ways that a son and brother can be.

It is unimaginable that I could only know or sense the brother that was before me, and beside me, and have no inkling that another Martin existed…

He was so clever and cagey at keeping us all in the dark… and out of his danger. He kept us in a bubble of protection. We were his family and I suppose he did not believe that we deserved to suffer the troubles he had gotten himself into.

As I loved planning and confiding in him, he too loved to still feel that he was integral to his family. I suppose my relationship with him allowed him to feel that way. The relationship was quite one-sided it seems. I provided cover for him and "took" from him.

There was very little, it seems that I would be capable of giving back.

Easter Sunday 1970: The test

EASTER SUNDAY IT should be warm outdoors but we are having one of those unexpected Spring snowstorms. I am not bothered by this as I had planned to be in all day cooking as I was having company for "Easter dinner" at our new apartment.

I had invited my brother to dinner that night and only Martin. My parents were off to a wedding ... the daughter of our old next door neighbor... and I don't know what was on tap for my sister.

I loved to cook and entertain and I always tried to make the meal a reflection of the company that was invited. I loved to "show off" how I had already mastered so many different techniques and cuisines. So with Martin as my guest, I naively thought that the dinner needed to be Italian. Why do I say naively? I understood so little about his life at that time that I took the fact that he was always in South Philadelphia (the Italian area of Philadelphia) to mean that he must now favor Italian food. My understanding of life, in particular his life, was that unsophisticated. I promised him an Italian feast.

I prepared manicotti with little meatballs in the sauce (we were not kosher in those days), a full antipasto and garlic bread and a home baked dessert. I spent the day in preparation and was pleased with the results.

Martin arrived at our apartment with a tall box. It contained a bottle of Galiano liqueur with two fancy glasses to drink it from. When I told him how much we appreciated the gift he was touched. Dinner was enjoyed by all.

After we had finished dinner we went to sit in the living room. This may have been the first time Martin came to this apartment, our first apartment, in spite of the fact that he had supplied and installed the wall to wall carpet as our wedding present. Sitting together on the sofa and love seat the topic came up about what my husband Heshie and I knew about "drugs." OK... so now he found us out...we knew nothing at all about drugs... except the kind a doctor prescribed when you were ill. Martin looked at the two of us as though we were from another planet. He pressed us... sure that we were not serious! "You mean you have never seen or tried marijuana?" The answer was an emphatic no. He went on to list a string of other illegal drugs. We had tried none of them. It was confirmed for him. He now knew for certain his sister was so "uncool." Perhaps he had been looking for an "in" with his sister and her husband? Or perhaps he even wanted to see if he could share some illicit activity with us?

We shared with him that Heshie had had his first alcoholic beverage on our honeymoon just months before. and Martin just laughed at that revelation. He could not understand that it was possible that we could have reached this time in our lives and been so inexperienced in all that he knew about the world and its illicit pleasures. I wanted to illustrate to my brother "just how good we were," so I shared with him this story:

"Martin, one of the teachers at the school where I am teaching science just had this same conversation with me and could not believe that I had never tried pot!! So she brought me a little bag of it to school and said it was a gift to usher Heshie and I into the "real world." So I nervously brought it home... and it lay around on my kitchen counter for several days. It began to make me so anxious even to have it in my possession that I took it into the bathroom and flushed it down the toilet! When my friend asked how I enjoyed the "pot" I admitted to her what I had done. She was as flabbergasted as you are, Martin! She was also quite angry at me for wasting such "good stuff." If I had not wanted to try it... she told me I should have returned it to her! That of course, would have necessitated me riding with it again in my car... and I was so fearful that I could be arrested for possession of an uncontrolled substance... that the toilet seemed the only solution that could keep Heshie and I safe! So Martin, there you have it... I have seen "pot," but I was so upset by having it in my home... I had to destroy it!"

He looked at me with incredulity... "what a pair my little sister and her straight arrow husband!"

While he questioned us, we did not question him as we didn't really even know the questions to ask. We weren't even curious about why he had quizzed us this way. We did not open the bottle of Galiano that night... and in fact we never did open it. It moved with us to every home that we lived in over the years. It is all I have that remains of my brother.

He left on that snowy night, amused and well-fed. I still did not understand that he lived in South Philadelphia at that point, not just because he liked Italian food and found it an exotic place to be (in comparison to living five minutes from our parents like we did)... but because it was the place in which he found the criminals that he now was involved with.

It is no surprise then that after he quizzed Heshie and I about our knowledge and use of drugs that there was no conceivable way to share with us anything about his real life.

Martin issued us a test... and we proved that we could not really know him. We now occupied two unrelated spheres of the world.

The Tower of Windsor Apartments: A second test

A BRAND-NEW COMPLEX in Cherry Hill New Jersey… several large "towers" of apartments and all the modern conveniences…

Martin moved here from his apartment in South Philadelphia to a brand new two bedroom two bath apartment on a high floor… with a view from his balcony.

Heshie and I visited as we were moving from our first apartment to a new apartment in Elkins Park. We had to move from that first apartment because I had had an unfortunate experience there one night when I came home from a class I was taking at Temple University. I was attacked by an assailant in our parking lot at knife point. The attack was thwarted… and I was safe, suffering only psychological trauma, but I never felt safe again in that apartment. We were forced to move.

So a new apartment meant new rugs, and new curtains… and this was Martin's department. He felt very upset about my experience and was eager to assure me that he could help with the transition to the new apartment in any way possible.

Heshie and I went to Martin's new apartment to discuss the new décor one evening after school . As we pulled up to Martin's complex… we were quite impressed that he was living in such a "fancy" place. The building had a doorman and a lovely lobby, it was a nicer place than any of us lived in. We assumed that this was a reflection of how well Martin was doing in his life.

Martin happily greeted us at the door of his apartment. We had never before been to any of his homes, so I did not know what to expect. The apartment was beautifully decorated, pastel wall-to-wall carpets throughout and lovely furnishings as well. He had a pastel sectional sofa with many multi-colored pillows scattered about on it. The dining room was furnished with a light wood table with chairs covered in a pink material. Everything blended together perfectly. Martin was proud to show us around, and finally in the second bedroom he introduced us to "my friend Joey" who was sitting by the desk. He didn't tell us why Joey was there that night. I suppose naïve Heshie and I just assumed that Joey was company, just as we were and that he had stopped over. Joey was "cute" very petite and slight and boyish. He seemed very sweet and he really did not interact with us very much. We had the chance to exchange pleasantries.

We reviewed all of the particulars of the new rugs and curtains... and then it was time to go...

A second test from Martin to Fredi, a second test failed: Martin was open to us meeting his "friend" Joey... and we asked nothing about it at all. He let us into his life, very briefly, really momentarily. Had we been more sophisticated maybe we would have seen what this friendship was all about(and it would have permitted me to talk to him about it)... but we were not, at all.

I am sure on the ride home to our apartment in Philly the conversation would only have dealt with how nice Martin's apartment was... and what good taste he had in his choices.

The Tower of Windsor Apartments...

Joey's mother had an apartment in that building as well and in the end Martin would allege that he paid for that one too.

Anthony De Pasquale, the supposed "hitman" in my brother's death moved into the same building just one month prior to Martin's murder, I am sure to case out his comings and goings.

Yes... the Tower of Windsor Apartments... this was where my brother died... in his car ... in the parking lot.

When he was good he was very good

WHEN HESHIE AND I married I was the support for our family. I began teaching in an inner-city school in North Philadelphia as a science teacher for seventh and eighth graders. Science was perhaps one of the last things these students really needed to be learning as it became quickly apparent that most of them students could not even read a textbook that dealt with science. Somehow I knew that I needed to adjust my teaching to allow the students to "experience" scientific principles rather than hear me drone on about them. I totally revamped the curriculum to be exclusively lab oriented and used my own funds to buy materials in order to do all of these experiments. I was mildly successful with my students and this was noticed by the department chairman and the Principal and in that first year they asked me to attend a science teachers conference in Atlantic City to present my ideas.

Heshie and I and another couple we were friendly with decided to make a weekend out of this and made plans to stay at a hotel in Atlantic City after the conference. It was all very exciting to me... the conference and the chance to stay in a hotel in a place that I visited often. I had always lusted after the chance to stay at the Strand, a place that I thought was so elegant. When the conference was over and I went to check in to the hotel I was told by the front desk that there had been an accident at home and that my friends were on their way to bring me back to Philadelphia, as my husband was with my mother who had been injured.

To say that I was close to my mother would be a gross understatement. My mother was central to every fiber of my being. I spoke to her daily expecting her to offer me her support and wisdom whenever I needed it. She was my sounding board for every aspect of life. The fear that this message injected into me was significant. How badly was she injured? What if she would not live? I could not even imagine my life without her in it. I had almost no experience with my mother being ill even... she may have had the flu once but she was the healthiest member of the family. I was a wreck!

My friends arrived shortly thereafter. They knew few details only that they were to bring me directly to the hospital where my mother was currently in surgery. There had been a car accident, my father was the driver, but only my mother was injured.

When we arrived at the hospital, I was greeted at the door by . Martin who had been the first to arrive there. Martin immediately embraced me and told me all that happened... my father of course was there too... but was waiting in the family room for my mother to come out of surgery. Martin's first words were that I should try to calm down... that he was "on this one" indicating that he would take the lead in assuring that all went well for my mother... and that he already had.

I sat with him waiting for word about my mother and Martin was running ahead very fast in deciding who needed to be called, what should be told, how things would be handled with my parent's business. He truly swung into action right before my eyes, and we sat together, united in vigil.

By the time my mother was in a room after surgery Heshie had also come back to the hospital from Medical school. We learned that mother's spleen had ruptured and so it was removed and that she was expected to make a full recovery. But having never even seen my mother sick it was shocking to all of us to see her with IV's attached and oxygen, and in pain. She was our strength, the bulwark of the family, we could not imagine her ill. Who would be there to take care of all of us? Who would protect us?

That night, I voiced my own fears, once again, to Martin. He assured me that mother would be alright, and that we all would make it through this, he intended to see to it! And it was his words and his comfort that allowed me to believe that this was so ... long enough to be able to go home with my husband that night and leave my mother's side.

When I awakened with terror at around four o'clock in the morning... I got up and got showered and dressed and explained to Heshie that I had to go back to the hospital to see that my mother was okay. He knew not to fight me on this… and I went and sat by her side She was glad to have my hand and my presence. It was not even daylight when we looked up and saw Martin come into the room. He, like me, was unable to sleep and had to be by mother's side. This same scene would repeat several more times until she was able to go home… he and I right by her side… and understanding the need for the presence of the other.

While my mother was still in the hospital, and right after this, Martin returned to the store to shoulder her responsibilities… as he said he would.

It was a rough time to have mother … not really like our mother… none of us were used to caring for her… she was the one always touching each of us. On one of the early morning visits I shared with her how hot it was outside and she motioned to the closet and told me to get her pocketbook out of it. She said: "In my wallet is my credit card. Take it and buy yourself an air conditioner for the apartment." That was my mother… that was what all of us depended upon and she could muster it even when she was in pain. And of course, my need was material and easy enough to rectify. Now I try to imagine this early morning scene with just mother and Martin… what could he say with honesty to her? What could he ask her to help him with? He was not so easy… an air conditioner would not suffice. My imagined words from him… " mother help me I've gotten myself in over my head with some very bad people." Nothing in her wallet could help with this. In fact, nothing in her motherly arsenal had ever been able to even touch this. Martin knew this well so he sat quietly… just holding her hand.

During the time that mother convalesced Martin bought her a silk, multi-colored, quilted robe to wear around the house. She treasured that robe more than words can properly say. It moved with her to every stop she made in life from that moment on. Once Martin died… the robe stayed in the closet and no one was permitted to touch it.

At the end of my mother's life when she had become very debilitated Jo Ann and I continued to do literally anything that we could imagine would make her happier and feel better. There were times during those years in particular… that I found myself missing Martin more than ever. It was the car accident that I would travel back to… and his embrace and his sentiment… that "I've got this one… relax"…

We needed him then to help with mother… his bond to her so strong. We needed him then to take part of the burden… and to hold both of us…

"You cannot be their savior!!!"

THESE WORDS TO me from my sister. In my second apartment in Elkins Park, I lived just ten minutes from my sister and her two boys, Ricky and Pauly.

When I finished teaching on most days I would rush home to my apartment to babysit for the boys so that Jo Ann could play tennis and do her errands. I loved this arrangement, as I thought there was nothing better in life than to be with Ricky and Pauly!! I planned activities for these afternoons together and sometimes they would help me to cook dinner and then I would feed them before my sister came to get them.

It was on one of these visits that I asked my sister to stay a few minutes at the end because I wanted her advice.

I remember that she and I each sat in front of a new "Martin set of drapes" in one of our matching green end chairs by the windows in my living room. We had taken the boys into my bedroom and sat them in front of Sesame Street... so that we could have a "talk."

I shared with my sister that Heshie and I were thinking about trying to have a child... and I wanted her opinion about whether she thought the "timing" was right for us to begin this process.

Jo wanted to know why I was in such a rush, as I was married for such a short period of time and Heshie was still in school. She had learned from her own experience that there was "no rush" on this, pointing out that Heshie and I were both very young.

And my rejoinder was: "Well... that's what you did and you have such great kids and I love every minute I spend with them. Oh and also... haven't you noticed how upset our parents are all the time? If, I could get pregnant and have another grandchild... maybe that would help to "cheer them up" and give them additional reasons for seeing life as positive."

Jo warned me: "If you and Heshie want to have a child you need to be doing this for the two of you and for the child! You cannot have a child to make their lives better you are not capable of fixing that situation. They are always having a problem with the business, and you know Martin makes them miserable, those forces are ones that you cannot impact. So if you want to have a child and it is best for you and Heshie, do it, but not for the reason you just offered me! You cannot be their savior"

I heard her words and thanked her for them and took them in, and then discarded them. I wanted to be a mother. I wanted Heshie and I to be parents. I was sure that my baby would be able to alleviate the sadness that I experienced from my parents all of the time. I was sure a new life was just what everyone needed most. And so, we got to work... and very quickly I was pregnant. The pregnancy preceded my knowledge of why Martin was making my parents so unhappy all of the time.

My parents were excited about another grandchild... as I expected they would be. Then the Spring of this pregnancy brought all of the reality of how bad things had gotten into stark relief.

My pregnancy could not cancel out all of the trouble that Martin was in. It could not save the family business. It was a blessing that the baby I was carrying was wanted and already loved by Heshie and I as I could see every day, that Jo Ann's advice had been correct.

And in the end, Julie would be born just in time for disaster to strike, and for Martin to be gone.

And she would... that first year... give my parents a reason to go on living.

So both sisters were correct on this one... each in her own way.

And in her way, Julie was our savior.

PART IV

Enlightenment: Our Eyes are Opened

The last time I saw him alive

Jo Ann

RECENTLY MY HUSBAND *reminded me that he was called by the Camden court to testify following Martin's murder. I had no recollection of that but he indicated it was the preface for his years of psychological distress. At the time he believed, rightfully, that he knew nothing of his brother-in-law's business practices in that he would have nothing valid to add to the proceedings.*

What we knew was what we read in the newspaper. I had no idea how involved my brother had become with mafia crime. The daily headlines screamed out to me and to my husband. The story they told was unfathomable... we found it too hard to accept or to discuss.

The Spring of 1972: A Study in contrasts. Who shall live and who shall die.

MY LIFE AND my brother's life in that time period were quite disparate. If one looks month by month at each of our lives the picture is crystal clear and eye opening. I was given life and a future with everything to look forward to; Martin was living with constant threat and the possibility that his life would end or be destroyed. As I traveled through these months I was oblivious to the danger my brother lived with daily. Two siblings... such differing outlooks...

Month	Fredi	Martin
February	I am beginning to look forward to being finished with my teaching stint in the Philadelphia School system. Heshie and I will probably be leaving Philadelphia for his residency... where we do not yet know.	Martin has been arrested and is working with his lawyer Joseph Santaguida to prepare for his trial in March. He is looking at possibly having to serve time in jail for his role in smuggling "hashish" into the country. In February... the family only knows bits of this story.

Month	Fredi	Martin
March	I am five months pregnant and all is going well. Heshie and I await word on which residency in pathology he has "matched" with. He hopes that he has landed a residency at Johns Hopkins Hospital as it is the most prestigious one in his field. March 15th comes. "match day"... he gets his first choice. We will be off to Baltimore to live and have a new home! We splurge and have an overnight to Baltimore to find a new apartment and we are successful in finding a beautiful one. Heshie is on course to be a leader someday in his field. This acceptance confirms that! In the later part of the month I find out about Martin's role in crime for real... for moments I hate what he has done this to our family!	My brother goes on trial for the smuggling case. My father attends this trial. In the midst of the trial, my brother threatens the life of his lover, Joey, out of frustration that the government has been turning people in Martin's life against him. My brother speaks passionately about their relationship in my father's presence. He is placed into prison on March 28th the first night of Pesach and it is in all of the Philadelphia papers and news channels.
April	We begin planning for our life in a new city. We are excited that we will live in a much nicer apartment with many amenities that we could not have afforded in Philadelphia. We are counting the days until graduation and then we leave to begin a new chapter of life.	With the advice of my parents and his lawyer my brother is convinced to turn "state's witness" in his case. With this decision he is released on bail until a later date for sentencing... if there will be sentencing after he testifies. It is confirmed to the judge that my brother has done all that was asked of him by the government.

Month	Fredi	Martin
May	It's graduation month for Heshie! We all attend his graduation at the Academy of Music and watch him become Dr. Harry Cooper, M.D. with honors. We celebrate this happy time with an open house at his parents' home.	My brother comes to the celebration of Heshie's graduation. He is not welcome there by my in-laws... but under protest from Heshie and me, he is allowed to come inside. During the visit we review with him the ins and outs of our new apartment and he assures that he will decorate it for us. We talk with him about our future but really don't know what to say to him about his future... and so avoid it. This is probably the time that my brother goes to talk with a prominent author, Gaeton Fonzi, about his "story" and asks him to cover it to help him find a way out.
June	I am in "moving mode" and very excited about everything in my life. We have worked with Martin to have new draperies and rugs made for the beautiful new apartment... and it will be beautiful when we are settled! We go to Jo Ann's house for a barbecue on Father's Day... the whole family is together. Martin assures us that everything will be ready in time for the move! (This will be the last time I will ever see my brother alive.) We leave for Baltimore at the end of the month and move in on June 31.	My brother continues to work with both his lawyer and with Fonzi to determine the best way to let his story be told out in the universe in hopes of finding a way to stop being harassed by both the mob and the government. His lawyer advises that he drop the idea of having Fonzi publicly tell his story now. He agrees to testify against the mob on August 7th. He works on my draperies and rugs and has them all ready in time for our move to Baltimore.

Month	Fredi	Martin
July	We have settled into our new home in Baltimore. It is beautiful and all of our choices are just right. When we arrive in Baltimore we buy a new kitchen set... and that too is exciting for us. Heshie begins his residency and loves it immediately. I meet a new doctor and quickly make new friends. We wait now for our baby to come. We explore our new neighborhood and we really feel like grown-ups for the first time... as we are on our own here and really starting off life together.	Sometimes during July, my brother lived in his apartment alone... sometimes his partner Joey was with him. Sometimes he lived with friends Paul and Candy Rubin in a house in New Jersey. He was doing business with Paul, and his own business... since he was going to testify... he was no longer doing business with the mob. The "hitman" moves into Martin's building in Cherry Hill... obviously to learn his pattern of coming and going to plan his demise. Martin is not aware of his presence.

And August says it all... I gave birth to my beautiful perfect baby, Julie on August the first. It was love at first sight. Everything I ever thought I wanted in life I now had... my intelligent, handsome, well-thought of husband, a lovely place to live, a loving family and now Julie too! Life was all that I could ever have imagined.

The day of Julie's birth I spoke to Martin for the last time. He was happy for us and excited about Julie. He was pleased that everything he had made for us had worked out so well. He was now days from testifying in court against the mob. We did not talk about that at all. I now know that he was terrified... and not sure he would live. He never told me this.

August 7th, I am home with my new daughter. He is on his way to court to testify.

He would never arrive. And I would never share life with him again.

Match day: Catching up to the truth

I WAITED BY the phone ready to find out our fate and on that day in mid-March my husband joyously called me and said: "let's get going I got into Hopkins!" Of course, he got into Hopkins. He had worked very hard all throughout Medical School and he had been mentored by a fine Pathologist and he was a prime candidate. Heshie got his first choice. We were so excited that it was recognized how talented he was. It was clear to me that he and thus our family were going to have a wonderful future together.

So I drove excitedly to Jefferson Medical School to pick him up our packed suitcase in the backseat of the Volkswagen Beetle. We had packed for an overnight trip "somewhere" as we hoped that he would get one of his two preferred choices... both of them away from Philadelphia.

Match Day 1972! An adventure for us! This was the city in which our first born would be born, breaking the family monopoly on being born in Philadelphia. This was really a "new beginning"... a first real step at adult independence for both of us. We would be on our own to really begin our lives together now... no parents living within five minutes of us... no extended family present at all times... new friends in a new place.

We checked into our hotel room and went to dinner in the hotel restaurant, called "the Pub." We decided we could really splurge on this dinner as a celebration. I ordered Prime Rib of Beef, one of my all- time favorites, and savored every bite of it. My obstetrician in Philadelphia watched every ounce of weight that a pregnant woman gained... but I threw caution to the wind! We were celebrating! I believe we each had a hearty piece of cheesecake, as well.

By the time we finally got back to our room my first order of business was to call my parents. I was eager to let them know that Heshie had gotten his first choice at the best program in Pathology in the country! I realized that they would actually dread us living "so far" from them in Baltimore but hoped they could at least feign happiness for us.

I dialed the phone and there was no answer. How was this possible that they would not be home by now? The store was closed an hour earlier and they always came right home. A bit of panic seeped in immediately. I took a deep breath and tried to wait another ten minutes before I tried again. Still, no answer. Now I tried the number at the store… feeling quite certain that they would not be there at this hour… there was no answer. My sense of panic was increasing. My mind was racing towards all kinds of terrible scenarios. They must be dead somewhere! I could not help myself from imagining this. I was all ready to call the police and report them missing. The joy of the day had quickly flown out the window.

Why panic? Why couldn't I just assume that they too had gone out to eat?

Panic was in the air a bit by mid-March of 1972. I did not know why, but everyone in the family seemed increasingly tense. My parents seemed to be sitting on a powder keg… but they consistently denied it. There never explained why they were so tense and ill- tempered.

So my sense that something was "off" with them was easily combined with the fact that they were not answering the phone when they told me to "be sure" to call them and let them know we had arrived safely and were OK. .

I tried calling again and had the same results. I did not want to call Jo as she would be busy with the boys. My choices at this point were to call my brother, my mother's sister or the police.

Heshie talked me down from the ledge where the police were concerned. He advised me to calm down and not assume something terrible had happened. So I took his advice and realized that I could call Martin. Perhaps he would know where they were and why I could not reach them.

I called him and shouted immediately that I had tried to get our parents repeatedly… as they had asked me to and I could not locate them. He said: "Calm down they were with me. We had some matters to discuss and so they came to me from the store. They just left my apartment and should be home in in forty five minutes. So try to settle yourself and call them at home then. "

I entreated him: "Is everything ok, is there some problem that caused them to come to you and stay so late?"

"No," he assured me. "There were just some things we needed to talk about. No need to ask them about any of it. It will all be fine, trust me."

So I thanked him profusely and then told him about the residency in Baltimore. I let him know we would be looking for apartments the next day. He promised me that he would be "my interior decorator" for our new home. I apologized for bothering him and getting all worked up about our parents. And he chuckled knowingly that this was just me being me where Mother and Daddy were concerned.

When I finally got my parents on the phone, I did not let on how crazy I had made my husband and myself trying to reach them. I was just relieved to hear their voices. I told them about our excitement and our fancy dinner and the nice hotel room. They listened patiently and said nothing about where they had been or why. I did not tell them that I had called Martin to find out where they had disappeared to. So they did not know that I knew they had been with him. They did not let on that there was a problem. They just "acted" happy for us and wished us success the next day in the apartment search.

We said a loving good night and I assured them that as soon as we got back the next day I would give them a rundown on the apartments in the running.

"Ok now," Heshie said, "we can go to bed and sleep securely knowing that your parents are safe and sound. Just try to relax."

So I did... but my unease merged with the rest of my family's. Something definitely was wrong. I guess I knew it was related to Martin, it always was.

After a successful hunt for a new home in a new city, we came home. The tension was still there. Maybe, I told myself, my parents were just upset because I was moving away... something that they could not fathom. Maybe, they could not tell me that this upset them so as not to hurt me or dampen my excitement about a new home and a new chapter... Maybe? Martin had said, don't worry, trust me! So I tried to do just that.

In just two weeks we would all learn what they were really upset about. Martin was in serious trouble now with the law. He would be arrested as a narcotics smuggler. I am sure that that night, the night I could not find them, they were with him... they were uncovering the truth about their son.

Soon the secret would be out and everyone would know.

The first night of Pesach, March 29, 1972. The big family seder at "The Falcon House."

THROUGHOUT MY LIFE to this date our family had a large, catered seder with all of my father's family… aunts, cousins, children… and people that had married into the family, as well. My father always conducted this seder from start to finish as he was the most knowledgeable about the seder and its meaning given his upbringing.

In March of 1972, I was excited about showing off my pregnant self to the entire assemblage at the seder. I was really "showing" now and I had gotten a new maternity dress… that I actually liked. It was a tweed dress interwoven with red, navy and yellow strands. Before going to sleep the night before I hung the dress out and took out the matching new navy blue patent leather pumps. This was a Pesach outfit redolent of the colors that I always had for my new spring outfit for the Seder. There would be relatives who had not yet seen me pregnant and that I might not see again now until after the baby was born… as Heshie and I were moving to Baltimore for his residency. It was such an exciting time for me… just the type of "story" to bring to the family seder and share with all of these people who had travelled through my life with me to this point.

The excitement of this upcoming event was not to be. When I woke up on March 29, 1972 I… all of the family was greeted by the story in the daily newspaper that my brother had been arrested in a crime "sting" concerning a drug smuggling ring… and that he had "talked" about a police officer who had been involved in this caper with him. This was the first that I knew anything about this… or perhaps the first that any of us knew about this. First I called my sister who was as panicked as I was. We were both sure that we would not have a seder this year. A call to my parents proved me wrong. My father insisted that the seder would go on as planned that night and that right now my parents did not want to discuss the trouble that had been revealed.

I ran first to my husband... alone in the study preparing for his last medical schools exams. I jammed the newspaper into his face and shouted:

"Now he has really done it! He has always been the source of trouble in our family... but never like this! I hate him I really do hate him! I just wish he would disappear!"

Never before in my life had I uttered such words about anyone. I could not believe that I was saying them about my own brother... I knew what I was saying was horrible... and yet I could not stop myself.... I wanted so much to be happy and to anticipate a happy future and he was assuring that this was not even possible.

"Martin"... I shouted to my husband..."I love him... he is my brother... I just don't even know what to say or think... no one I know had ever had a problem like this one... how will we all manage?"

Heshie said nothing to this outburst from his young wife... he just held me... and listened. He would be the only one ever to know that I had said things so uncharacteristic of me... hatred mixed in with love.

Here... read it... take it all in... as I pushed the paper at him...

The headlines read: "Unnamed Cop Is Linked to Hashish Probe... and in it we learned that Lt. Joseph Marker... alleged to be a "big man in the Police department" may have been involved in a plot to smuggle 185 pounds of hashish into the country last year." (March 29, 1972, The Evening Bulletin). The article went on to identify my brother as the other man involved in this plot with Lt. Marker. It was also noted in this article that a special agent had identified my brother as an informant... earlier in the year identifying other suspects... to Lt. Marker who ironically served on the narcotics squad. I further learned in this article that this was not "new" activity for my brother. He had been connected to and working with Marker since April 1969... which would be the season in which I was preparing for my wedding... and would spend time with my brother more regularly... without any hint that anything was awry for him then.

A second column on that same page related to my brother appearing before federal judge Thomas Masterson, and the judge asking a witness if my brother had threatened to "kill him." The witness, Joseph Conti admitted to the judge that my brother had threatened not only "Joey" but his mother as well. When Joey was asked if he was frightened by my brother he answered the judge... that he was. Joey was that sweet friendly guy who my brother said was his 'friend." I was so clueless at the time that I had no idea that Joey was anyone of significance in my brother's life.

If it was news to my parents, Jo Ann and I... of course the larger extended family and in-laws were also learning of this for the first time. How could we come to the seder and face any of them? That was the first question, for that day, beyond my father's visit to my brother in jail. We worried more about the seder and less about how that visit had gone for my father, beyond my father's visit to my brother in jail.

It was a horrible night. I arrived in my "Pesach outfit" not ready to look into the eyes of anyone who was in the room... and no one wanted to look into my eyes either. We were all consigned to go through the motions of the seder, reading of the plagues in the Exodus story, with a huge "unnamed plague" present at the seder table... just as the seder plate adorned the table. My father stood and intoned without any feeling or emotion every word; he was like a zombie. We were hearing the Passover story...while this other nightmarish story hung in the air. My mother could not really sit at the table at all, and at one point my sister and I realized that she was missing and we went to find her passed out in the ladies room. She could not cry or even talk... she had not eaten a morsel all day. We got her to drink and got her back on her feet. She would not rejoin my father at the table, she could not face our closest family.

There were really no words that any of us could say to anyone. We were all in a state of shock. This was the first open knowledge that we had that Martin had really entered into something from which there was no return. We knew he was erratic, that he had problems, that he seemed troubled, and yet we also knew him as our brother, our son, and interacted with him... we thought... openly. We found out that he had become "enslaved" to a pharaoh that we could not recognize at all. He was like a foreigner to us as of that day, how could he have threatened the life of another?

Pesach 1972…would be a foreshadowing of the plague of darkness and death of the firstborn…when we "read" the story that night…we began to understand… that we would not taste freedom in the weeks and months ahead. Martin was in a prison and we were going through the motions…this time God would not "let this people go."

And I pray that God had not heard me say…" I hate him… I just wish he would disappear…"

My fear that day, What if my words had power?

Caught in a trap...and he takes the rap

IT WAS AN elaborate scheme for smuggling hashish into the country from as far away as Afghanistan. There is no question that my brother had some involvement in this scheme. There are questions however, about who else was involved and why exactly was Martin the one who took the rap... mainly. It is also clear that my brother had no idea that the government knew about this elaborate scheme and that they were "following his every move" and that they would "get him." Perhaps he thought he was safe because one of the "characters" that he had been doing business with for years was a member in good standing with the Philadelphia Police Department, Lt. Joseph Marker.

This was Martin's first trial in March of 1972. My father was the only family member to attend. I was teaching school at this time. My sister was busy raising her two little boys. My mother was at the family business. It embarrasses me to admit that none of us understood that Martin's entire family should have shown up to show our support for him. We were ignorant then of what a misguided decision this was.

From US Court records the opening argument of the Prosecutor states:

"The evidence from the witness stand will clearly show that on or about the first day of May 1971 a Land Rover, which is a large automobile, or a small truck, used generally for driving in the desert, was shipped from Africa containing approximately 185 pounds of hashish, which is a drug. The evidence will show that that vehicle eventually landed up in Philadelphia, and that Martin Alan Hess attempted to get into possession of that vehicle and attempted to get possession of the drugs inside. You will learn that he had the shipping documents, the keys, the registration for the vehicle, and he was arranging with people in Philadelphia to get that vehicle to turn over the hashish to other individuals."

My brother's attorney, Joseph Santaguida would argue in Martin's defense that:

"Now the Land Rover in question, this truck, or van that had the marijuana in it, originated in Africa and was shipped from Africa to New York. Now, Mr. Hess had no knowledge of the Land Rover or the hashish. You will find that that will be the unanimity of the evidence. The person who owned the van and who owned the hashish, he will testify that he is in prison now because of this, and he will say that, "This was my idea, this was my truck, I pled guilty and I am now doing six months in prison. You will hear from this man himself that Mr. Hess is not the person who contracted him to get this hashish off the Land Rover. The person who contracted and who he contacted was Philip Viner.

"Now for some reason the Government has chosen not to arrest Mr. Viner. Mr. Viner is not charged with this particular crime, even though Mr. Warner has told the government and he will tell you that Mr. Viner was the person whom he hired to get the marijuana and hashish off of the Land Rover.

"Now you will hear testimony from the U.S. Customs Agent who had this Land Rover under surveillance for two to three days while in Philadelphia. They will also tell you that he was in the company of someone else, a Philadelphia police officer, a Lieutenant police officer. They know this but the police officer was never arrested... and we don't know why?

"You will hear from one Ragillio Fontaro arrested several times, and convicted of crimes. He was the one contacted to tow the Land Rover from where it was parked at 8th and Market and drive it to his garage so he could take the marijuana and hashish from the Land Rover. He agreed to do this and was never arrested by the government... even though the government knew of his involvement in this crime... and why? We do not know.

"We want to know why these other people, just as implicated were not arrested, why they want you to come back and say Martin Alan Hess is guilty of this crime... and none of them are?

"The government will also show that anything that Mr. Hess did was done in the open and in the accompaniment of a Philadelphia Police officer.

"We will bring character witnesses that will testify that Mr. Hess is a law-abiding citizen never before involved with breaking the law. He has a good reputation... an excellent reputation.

"Later in this testimony the two lawyers interrogate the Customs official who followed the car from its inception point in New York to the garage in Philadelphia. The agent had watched the vehicle for a complete day when it was parked in a garage in Philadelphia. When the garage locked up he left and came back the next day to resume his surveillance. He claims that he was in the Lit Brothers Parking lot when he first saw "Mr. Hess and another gentleman approach the vehicle. He reported: "I saw the two of them stop at the vehicle, look at the vehicle, never touched it but looked at the vehicle... and then gazed around and kept walking around.

"Was this the first time you ever saw Mr. Hess?

"Was the gentleman that you saw that day looking at the Land Rover, the same many you see in the courtroom today?"

"Yes sir."

And believe it or not that is the point where the testimony for this agent stopped and the court was adjourned. Overnight there would be another development that would need attention in the court the next day... and this is the place where the records end in my search.

It seems that Martin was carrying all of the guilt for this plot alone... perhaps except for the owner of the Land Rover. Other names were mentioned... and somehow the government had given them a pass... Martin was the leader of this plan! In some way... this seems laughable... as he was clearly involved with career criminals and a very bad acting police officer. Somehow they all... and I believe the government too... had placed him in the "hot seat"... and let him be the main actor in a scheme that was clearly above his knowledge level... or sophistication in matters such as these.

Uncovering, discovering, and still hearing Martin

IN THE RESEARCH that I have undertaken there are many articles related to my brother and to the people he had associated with that caused his ultimate undoing. The articles unmask a side of Martin that I did not know... that none in the family knew and yet embedded in them there is truly my brother that I loved and at times hated.

I read an article in the *Philadelphia Bulletin* dated July 12, 1972 and the tears came readily. It is an account of my brother's testimony in a trial against police officer, Lt. Joseph Marker. After Martin supplied crucial and incriminating evidence in Common Pleas court, "Judge Latrone strongly admonished Hess that if anyone approached him 'I want to know in ten seconds... my number is in the phone book.'" But then the judge decided to order Hess to spend the night in the Adelphia Hotel in the company of court officer Frank Spino.

What caused my tears? Hearing my brother's words of response. Martin implored the judge that he had drapery customers to see that night. That he had an obligation to those customers for service and that he would prefer not to disappoint the customers by not delivering what they were expecting. The judge agreed to allow my brother to see those customers that night but he had to have Mr. Spino along for the trip. Ultimately, they all agreed on this plan.

This raised so many questions for me. One night's custody because of his testimony? Surely that was like putting a band-aid on a large surgical incision! If there was concern that what my brother had revealed placed him in jeopardy why wasn't a real plan of protection undertaken?

My heartbreak and my tears are in response to the other part of my brother, that I actually knew. While deep in testimony about a drug plot that he too had been implicated in... he worried about his responsibility to his customers. In his words, I recognized something that I know well about myself. I have lived this script and always deliver on it... if a promise is made to another it is important/necessary to fulfill this promise. My brother... the one I knew also had this in his psyche somewhere... and it was reflected in his first words to Judge Latrone. He understood that the judge was concerned about his welfare and yet he was concerned about the customers.

Martin fought the family's conventionality and said that he would never embrace it... and yet... within his soul the lessons and the values did have a place and he could not turn his back on them. I imagine that he was constantly at war with the competing forces in his life. He had entered a culture that was aberrant to everything that he had been exposed to in his biological family. The crime family held a compelling allure for him. And yet, the lessons of his actual family still required him to do the "right thing" for others. This desire to do the right thing and the dictum from my parents to do the "right thing" would actually not really work with the culture of organized crime. This part of Martin, trying to do the right thing in a world where this is alien, would be his final undoing.

Judge Latrone knew he was in danger, and yet could not properly translate the gravity of the situation to my brother.

I cry because of his innocence in this regard, not fully understanding just how deep the danger was for him now. I cry because we, his family, were blind to understanding this. Finally, I cry at reading the words of the judge for the realization that the system was so willing to take his knowledge and information from him, but made such a feeble attempt to protect him for "doing the right thing."

Of all the things there were, this was what he did not want us to know

WHAT WAS MY brother most worried that we would discover?

Martin worried that we would find out about the love in his life. Why would he keep this from us? Wouldn't we want to know that he was loved and cared for by another? It was 1972, and in 1972 he knew that this too was something that his family would consider taboo. Martin was in love with and lived with a man for over four years.

At the trial I hear my brother as he answers questions about why in anger he may have threatened the life of this man...Joey Conti...and my heart breaks at his words:

Q. *Mr. Hess, you know Mr. Conti. Is that correct?*

A. *Yes.*

Q. *How long have you known him?*

A. *About six years. We have lived together four years.*

Q. *Did you visit him yesterday?*

A. *Yes.*

Q. *Tell us what happened when you went to visit him.*

A. *I went to visit him to find out, you know, why he was going to be a witness in this case. I wanted to find out what the reason was, because Mr. Conti... over a long period of time was, you know, a very good friend of mine, you know... and I could not understand how he could be, you know, be on the side of Mr. Miller, because he was... he understood everything about it and he knew everything that happened in the case, and he was my closest friend. And I was amazed to hear yesterday that he would have anything to testify against me.*

Q. *Now, when you first went to visit Mr. Conti, did you speak to him the way you are speaking now? In a regular tone of voice?*

A. *Yes. I went to see him to try to find out what he was talking about, what he wanted to say, because he told me many, many times that he felt sorry for me. That he wanted to try to help me and show, you know, who the really guilty people were in this case and that was his objective. And it has been all through this year that Agent Winburn and Agent Moss have harassed my life and Mr. Conti's life... have made it impossible for either of us to live... and have created situations such as occurred yesterday, constantly in my life since my arrest. And they have caused Mr. Conti to become an enemy of mine in the past month. They set him up to make recordings of me and things like this. This was the one person that was very close to me, and he knows that I would never hurt him, and I know that he would never hurt me, that he would only hurt me on behalf of Agent Winburn. He is not sharp enough to realize what these people are doing to him and to me.*

Q. *Let me say this to you. Was there something that he said that infuriated you after you had somewhat of a conversation?*

A. *The only thing he said is that he wanted to testify at the trial so that he could let the truth be known so that he could tell the jury who the real people were in the back of the case, you know, and I told him---I asked him, "Didn't I suffer enough this year? Why should other people suffer? Why would you assure that the other people who love me have to suffer too?"*

A. *Definitely. What more can I say?*

Q. *Is there anything about your personal relationship that you felt would be embarrassing to you or to your family?"*

A. *Definitely there was; it was hard for me all around.*

Later on cross examination by the prosecutor, there was an even clearer picture of the pain my brother was experiencing.

Prosecutor: *Mr. Hess why didn't you work through your lawyer? Why didn't you have Mr. Santaguida contact Mr. Conti... or contact us?*

My brother: *A: I will tell you something. When you live with somebody for four years, or five years of your life... if you have to talk with them about something... I don't think there is any reason why you can't go and talk to them. I lived with Mr. Conti, nor would Mr. Conti have to go to an attorney to see me... he spent the last weekend in my apartment. I can only say to you last night that I was very upset with Mr. Conti... I really in my emotion... I could not tell you what I said to Mr. Conti...*

The Judge: *Mr. Hess, what made you so upset last night particularly?*

A: *Mr. Conti was supposed to be called by my lawyer, Mr. Santaguida, to testify on my behalf. And then it all turns around. Mr. Winburn apparently got to Mr. Conti first. He said on tape that he would testify on my behalf... if you ask him now, you know, he will tell you that he wants to explain to the jury that I was a stooly in this matter. And now, he comes with these people who have been trying to lynch me for the last year... he becomes now part of their case against me.*

And later... his attorney asks: *Mr. Hess, was the fact that you were apprehensive certain personal relationships were to become public... did that infuriate you... that you felt Mr. Conti would testify about this?*

And so there it was in his voice—Martin was worried that we would know that he loved a man and that a man loved him. And he was so agitated over this and all of the ways that he had been manipulated in this process that he shouted in anger to his lover words that had no real meaning at all, except his anger and his fear of everything about him being known to us. My father sat there and heard all of this. He heard his son acknowledge his lover and his fear that his family would know about this. My father, from a traditional Jewish background, one raised firmly believing the biblical text Leviticus 18 that it was an abomination for a man to lie with a man. My father heard it and I feel certain, yet one more time that he believed his son, his first born son, was an abomination. Better to just sacrifice him than allow this to continue!

Martin clearly loved Joey, and when further questioned he said:

"Mr. Conti knows that I would never harm him and I know that I wouldn't harm him. I was angry with him and he would stand in this court and say these things about me? He knows that I am not capable of hurting him or his mother. The only person that hurts people is the agents of the government that causes these terrible situations with people who love each other."

These words are like a knife in my hearts. Martin, I wish I could have helped you. I wish I could have let you know that I would understand. Forty-five years later—such a different time—so much of what had fueled his life off course then is well embraced today.

The last time I ever saw him

IT WAS FATHER'S Day 1972 and my sister was having all of us over for a Father's Day dinner.

I can picture all of us at that dinner around my sister's dining room table. Jo Ann had already achieved all that I dreamed of in life... two children and that "single house" in suburbia. No doubt she had barbecued on her outdoor grill... hot dogs, hamburgers and chicken. Her two boys Ricky aged four and Paul aged three were very much the center of attention. We were all in our "barbecue mode and attire."

And then in walked my brother Martin.

Martin arrived at the dinner in a grey silk suit, dressed to the nines. He also came bearing gifts, not for his father but for the two boys. I can picture a big stuffed brown bear riding toy that he brought for them. They were so excited. It was so Martin. When he walked into the room he commanded the attention to shift to him, sometimes in a negative way, but that day in the sweet and loving way that he was also capable of.

Martin was already in trouble. He had been in jail that Spring and was now out and trying to live his life. What did I know of that life at all? I knew that again the sweet and generous Martin was in charge of having two rugs made for me for my new apartment, one for my dining room and one for Julie's room, and to have the carpets he had given us for our previous two apartments made into area rugs. He assured me that day that the rugs would all be ready in time for the moving truck which would be leaving Philadelphia the next week, and he made good on that promise!

But there must have been so much more on his mind that day than my rugs and even the mundane life that his two sisters were living. At that time he was into organized crime so deeply that he lived in fear for his life, but none of us sitting around the table could know or understand that. He shared very little of it with us; he carried it by himself. Ironically, I was to learn in doing my research for this memoir, that in "his world" he talked way too much about who he was involved with and what he knew about their escapades. The gangsters considered my brother a braggart. But when he entered our world, so diametrically opposed to his, there was little he could open to us. He knew our predictable textbook middle class life, because he had lived a version of it. Yet we knew absolutely nothing of his. He was scared and we were unable to help him. He sat with us and "celebrated" yet he was apart from us. His world and ours in stark contrast.

When I said good-bye to him that night, how could I know that I would never see him again? I spoke with him before I left Philadelphia to thank him for all of the trouble he had gone to with the rugs and regal curtains for our new baby's room. I so appreciated that he got them to us just in time. There would be only one more time I would hear his voice and that was five weeks later. I was in Baltimore now starting my new life. I called to tell him about Julie the day that she was born. He was happy for me and wished all of us well. By this time he knew he was staring down the barrel of the gun, as in less than a week he would testify against some of his associates. We did not discuss what was coming up for him or how he was feeling. I lacked any vocabulary to talk with him about his life. It was foreign to me. I had only one version of him in my mind and in my heart. I always had hoped that this idealized version would come to fruition. I hoped that he would finally wake up and realize that the way we were brought up was not really so bad after all, and that he could actually be a true part of our family. Oh if only he could have let himself know us, and that we could have known all of him, and that judgement and disapproval on both sides could have dissipated.

In a few weeks he would be gone.

Equation for success circa 1969

SUCCESS = COLLEGE + Acquiring a husband (preferably one on a professional pathway or rich), which leads to: Home + children+ greater wealth than the parents had.

I was good at math, so the equation which had been drummed into my head took hold and I worked to solve it throughout college. It seemed that I was totally on the right pathway.

After the "Goodbye Columbus" wedding, Heshie and I settled down into our new life. I was beginning a teaching position in an inner-city Philadelphia school as a Science teacher. I was also attending Temple University at night to obtain the degree that would allow me to teach as my newly minted Liberal Arts degree was insufficient to provide the proper requirements needed to be a teacher. I had no way of knowing that I was a natural born teacher, but I was, and even in the extremely challenging setting I taught in I had instincts of how best to reach students in seventh and eighth grade who could not read past a second grade level—who needed me to teach them science. I entered this position as a way to support Heshie and me as he was a full-time medical student. So it was all pragmatic. I would work through his years in medical school, then have a baby at graduation time, and then become the "doctor's wife" and stay at home. A perfect solution to the above-mentioned equation.

Heshie was extremely happy and successful in his studies at Jefferson Medical School and had grown close with his "cadaver mate"...Joel. Happily, I knew Joel's, wife, Bonnie, from our old neighborhood and so the four of us became quite inseparable.

One day Bonnie's parents invited all of us to their Center City apartment, for brunch. This would be my—our (Heshie's and my)—first foray into seeing up close "how the folks who made it really lived!" We were greeted at the door by a maid who saw us to the table. The apartment was beautiful, airy and large. They actually had made it a two story apartment. The table was overflowing with food and we were warmly greeted by Bonnie's parents. They wanted to get to know this couple who had spent so much time with their children. And the father—the doctor was anxious to meet Heshie as Joel had raved to him about how bright he was. The conversation was easy and comfortable and "visions of sugar plums" danced in my head ("This is what my life might be some day!"). Myra, Bonnie's mother did not have to busy herself in the kitchen as the maid did it all for her. She just sat and took part in the brunch. What a luxury. It was all a luxury.

But wait... then Myra began to talk about her own professional life. She was the director of a burgeoning program at Hahnemann Hospital in Art Therapy. She was the ground-breaking founder of this entire new field and she was erudite and eloquent in describing all of the projects that were unfolding for her.

The equation? She had not totally adhered to it; she went beyond its boundaries.

I was instantly intrigued by her. I heard the script in my head saying, "Oh she is a doctor's wife; she did not have to work. They have plenty of everything without her income. Yet she has talent and she has pioneered something on her own!"

She reminded me a bit of my mother: thoughtful, intelligent, well-spoken, the brains in the family.

Yet my mother had not been able to do what Myra had; she had not married the doctor and then found a way to pursue her own path. She was stuck every day in the Godforsaken hell of the family business. My mother was the CEO of Tacony Curtain and Linen, a working woman of substance at a time when women did not work, but yet she had taught me that damned equation, not taking into account that had she had the chance to pursue her own pathway, she too would have been a Myra.

So I left brunch that Saturday with something I did not expect. It was not the salad or the dessert or the maid waiting on all of us or even the beautiful apartment. I left reworking the equation.

In the short time I had already spent in that inner city Philadelphia Junior High School I had had a taste of knowing I had talent as a teacher and that I had something to offer children and others too... Myra started me thinking for real now about "what else could I do... in addition to being the doctor's wife?" Maybe someday I would be more than the wife at home with the babies... I drank it in... and then knew that those "stupid courses" I was required to take at Temple University in order to maintain my teaching position... actually might be something I should be paying attention to... maybe they would offer me some idea of where and how to determine who I might be... all on my own.

After this brunch I began to take seriously that I could alter the equation and land more solidly in life than I had been programmed for. This was just a first step.

Meanwhile I realize that my brother had also been exposed to an equation, and at this very time he was trying to solve the "getting rich" part in his own way. He was also finding that the ordinary solution to the equation was not going to work for him either.

Equations—How can we work through them to come up with our own creative solutions?

I had mine.

Martin had his.

Mine added up to something ultimately.

His added up only to trouble.

Both of us were trying to solve that piece of "reach beyond" who we were raised to be.

Success = Figure it out for yourself!

What happens if you think you can be a part of the underworld?

"A spokesman for the government said there is no doubt Hess had been dealing with 'some very tough individuals in the narcotics field.' Most of his activities, the spokesman said, were in New York."
—The Philadelphia Inquirer, *August 8, 1972*

SOME VERY TOUGH individuals.

Martin was like a "little boy" who wanted to play with the big bullies and so tried to "act" like them... until it was clear to that little boy that he really needed to run home to find safety.

Somehow some of the "other boys" who had gotten involved like my brother had in this operation either knew the rules of the game better than he did or had connections that could buy them safety that my conventional Jewish family knew nothing about.

The architect of the hashish smuggling escapade was not my brother at all. It was a man by the name of Stephen Warner.

In his testimony he recounted his trip with his wife Andrea to Europe and Africa. He told of the purchase of the drugs and of the purchase of the Land Rover that would conceal the drugs. The trip to possess the drugs and the vehicle took him to Afghanistan, Africa, Denmark and then London. He also recounted the manner in which the Land Rover was outfitted so that the drugs could be concealed. He reported on the manner in which he and his wife provided for the transport of the vehicle by boat from London to New York. Finally, he and his wife met the Land Rover in New York and drove it to Philadelphia and parked it in the fateful garage in which my brother would be seen inspecting the vehicle.

Somehow with all of his involvement... Mr. Warner spent only six months in prison... and the overall responsibility for this caper was charged to my brother's ledger.

There were other "nice Jewish boys" involved in this scheme as well. The rest of them did not have to pay with their lives.

In the same federal trial Alan Diamond testified about money that was given to my brother. He characterized Martin as a simple "go between"... in the middle between Warner and Lt. Joseph Marker. He reported that he worked with Joseph Viner, and Jeffrey Dukow and they met with my brother to give him money for Marker. The prosecution uncovered in questioning Alan Diamond that he and Viner sold marijuana on the street.

Another witness that day, Alan Freedman, told how he had been with the Warners in Afghanistan when they took possession of the drugs. He was a 50-50 partner in the smuggling operation with the Warners. Freedman stated that he got involved with this operation out of greed, and he too served six months in prison for his part.

Both Viner and Dukow were able to work out a plea bargain with the government in exchange for their testimony.

And then there was a Norman Felt... and Paul Rubin... who also testified...

All Jewish guys... probably from similar middle class backgrounds, some of them actually college educated. Somehow they, and their families, knew what to do to keep them safe... even though they were as guilty... or guiltier than Martin.

No man's land... He stood between forces that pulled him hither and yon... one side plotting to get him in one way... while the other side plotted how to bring him down another way... he was there with no way out.

One side... the mobsters met to plot his murder

The other side... the government agents met to determine who to "get to" in his life to turn against him.

He stood in the midst of this... recognizing both how stuck he was and also in how much danger he was in and he hoped that the "men in the white capes (in other words the government agents) would eventually help to save him from this death grip that he was living in.

From court records I share the two sides that had him just where they needed him:

The Mob:

"On February 2, 1973, Charles Grubert, a special agent for the FBI, received a telephone call from Frederick Schiavo, a defendant. In the course of the conversation, Schiavo said he had information concerning the murder of Hess, and would provide this information to the Government in return for the FBI's help in another, unrelated matter.

"John Florio, a man not unfamiliar with the law, knew the defendant from their boyhood days in South Philadelphia. Since Labor day of 1971, Florio had seen the defendant at least a dozen times in Atlantic City, at the Marriot Hotel outside of Philadelphia, and at a private home in Philadelphia. On several of these occasions when the defendant, Florio, and others were present discussions took place about the planning for the murder of Martin Hess."

So this despicable group of mobsters met repeatedly, more than eight of them, to carefully plan my brother's murder. Martin knew he was in mortal danger and had no way to get anyone to help him to extricate himself from this vice.

In the Spring before his death he was in prison for the drug smuggling case. My parents visited with him there on several occasions and reported to me that they hoped that Martin would turn "state's witness" in this case to win his own freedom. Martin tried to explain to them that this would put his life in danger, but they hoped that he would be a "mensch" and make this ugly chapter close by "doing the right thing."

While Martin suspected the danger he was in, it was difficult for him to know how best to protect himself, and this became evident in reviewing records from the bail hearing in his case .

Martin stood before the judge and heard the prosecutor share with the judge just how helpful my brother had been now for the overall case. He shared that while Martin was in prison, he had done the "right thing" and offered the government a great deal of information in order that they could continue to prosecute the "bigger fish" in this matter. My parents had appealed to Martin, and somehow he determined that he would make his wrongs disappear if he did what was asked of him.

But then the judge asked my brother if he thought that his life was now in danger. Here is that interchange:

Federal Agent: *Your honor, Mr. Hess had indicated he will cooperate in this matter in any way that is needed. As far as his safety is concerned we are concerned over two things; one is his physical safety; and secondly, we want to have Mr. Hess feel assured he is safe on the street. In that regard, Mr. Hess has not been very specific as to what he would like us to do. We are prepared to go to any extent which Mr. Hess feels he needs, plus our independent examination of the situation. We have the cooperation of both the Philadelphia Police Department and the U. S. Attorney's office and the Customs Agents. As far as manpower is concerned, we will give Mr. Hess any amount of protection he would like to have.*

Judge: *Now Mr. Hess, what concerns if any, do you have about your safety?*

Martin: *I am concerned with my safety but I don't know what type of protection to ask for.*

Judge: *Well the District Attorney and the US attorney have indicated that they are willing to give you whatever protection you want... it seems it is up to you to tell them what you want.*

Martin: *Judge I will be very honest with you. I don't even understand what is possible in this regard. No one has adequately told me this. This is their business, not mine. I don't even know how they do it.*

Federal Agent: *I think, perhaps, Your Honor, we could work this out with Mr. Hess. He may be in a clearer state of mind once he is released from custody and is posted on bail. We would like him to be safe without any restriction on his movement... but I think we can work this out with the prosecutor.*

And then the court was dismissed... the "good guys" had a cooperating witness... he had given them the beginnings of what they wanted and needed... and they were not terribly concerned about really "locking down" a means of keeping Martin safe.

He told them in clear words that he did not really know how they kept a cooperating witness safe... and all that was determined was that they would work on it.

Both sides... getting what they wanted from him...

One side determined to do him in

The other side voicing concern... but not willing to put anything in place

No way out.............

After my brother's death the Judge told a reporter:

"When I released Hess on bail last May he thought government agents were going to keep Hess on ice until all of these cases were over. When he was released from here, I was assured by the U. S. Attorneys that he would be protected. Hess' death is the assassination of a key witness in several Federal and local cases."

U.S. Attorney Carl Melone refused to comment on the Judge's remarks. But a customs officer said... Hess chose not to avail himself of the offer... he wanted to do his own thing."

A lame excuse in my book for a complete dereliction of duty by the government... my brother's blood all over their hands.

A lifetime of guilt for saying no

MARTIN WAS NOW in jail and my parents had visited him there several times. Each visit made them physically and emotionally ill and they both were visibly depleted. Mother came to my apartment after one of those visits and shared how horrific it was to see her son in prison garb. The ordeal was more than they could take.

So here comes the request from my mother, my heart, and my lifelong soul double and confidante:

"We have used up all our money on his defense and you know that the store has gone into bankruptcy so that is no longer a source of easily accessible cash. Can you and Heshie help us to fund his bail?"

It was like a punch in my gut—can we help to fund the bail? Who were we? I did not know how we could be seen as a source of cash!

- Heshie was in his last two months of Medical school so he made nothing at all
- I was in my last two months as a teacher in the Philadelphia School system, and every penny I made went to pay our rent, utilities, car payment, insurances, and food. There was never a cent left.
- We had exactly four thousand dollars in the bank, and that was meant to be used to move us to our new home in Baltimore, pay our first, last, and security deposit on a new apartment, and also a tiny cushion to cover the fact that a resident's salary at Johns Hopkins Hospital was even less than the pittance I was paid teaching.

I had to say no to my mother... I am sure that was the one and only time I ever did in my life... but I did it! And then, I began immediately to strategize with her about how my parents could get the money...who they were more likely to be able to ask and have them say yes. (Jo Ann tells me that she was never asked to help with this, but had she been she too would have said no.)

The usual suspects:.

My father's sisters in Atlantic City... Lil and Gert... they were the ones who literally "bailed" anyone in the family out of financial difficulty if they were in need... -My mother's sister Shirley and her husband Abe...

After we hatched the obvious plan I could breathe again... they would get the money... Martin would get out of jail on bail... I would not be the financial helper... but maybe I helped a little?

I carried that "no" with me for a long time... how could you be so selfish to put your needs first in such a dire season? I truly believed that I could not tax our newly expanding family in sharing our little savings account with my parents... but it was my parents and my brother... they needed something from me... and I could not offer it... I also felt somewhere inside myself that this would be money flushed down the toilet... as they had spent so much money getting Martin out of trouble over the years... this would just be one more of those occasions... Money spent... no noticeable result.

And yet, could I have made a difference here had I taken that leap and given the money to them—to him?

It is so unlike the person I have become over the years that I hardly recognize myself telling mother "no."

I would jump to answer her every need from August 7, 1972 on, never saying no again—never. Even up to her dying day, if she asked, she got it immediately, whatever it was—no expense was ever spared. At times my life could be consumed with assuring that mainly my mother was happy. If I sensed a bad tone in her voice I would immediately inquire what was wrong. If it was within my power to correct the problem I did so ASAP. When it was time for my mother to move out of her apartment and live in an assisted community... my sister and I chose the nicest one around. Mother had no money to live there... but we wanted her to be happy, and comfortable and we did whatever was necessary to assure that this was so. The irony... that when my parents needed 4000 dollars thirty years before... I could not say yes.

My sister and I absorbed literally hundreds of thousands of dollars to allow mother to live her life to the end like a lady. I had lunch or dinner with her at least once a week at her community and when she smiled... it was worth every single cent that was spent. On a day when she was unhappy... I left in tears feeling that somehow... my efforts had been insufficient to lift her mood. At the end of dinner if mother said: "I cannot find my white pants and I need them"... I was off to the mall on the way home to assure that the next day I would deliver several pair of new "white pants."

In the end of her life when she said, "Do not let me die alone with no one at my side," I heard her request and took it in, and when the time came for mother to go on hospice care in the hospital, we both actually entered hospice. I took her request quite literally—she in the bed and me in the chair beside her. She was not conscious at this point but I could not/would not leave her side. I held tightly on to her hand with every breath that she took. When nature called—and I had to use the bathroom in her room—I would tell her, "I am just going to the bathroom mother. I will be back momentarily. Don't go anywhere without me." She and I traveled this way for eight long days and nights. I would quickly shower in her bathroom, also telling her my whereabouts. When mother took her last breath, I was right there where she had asked me to be, holding her hand. With that last breath I finally felt vindicated for that uncharacteristic "no" I had uttered so many years before. Mother had asked, and I had been able to do what she most needed. She was my heart, and I tried my best then to give her mine.

That fateful Marriot meeting

IN OUR SHELTERED existence our family knew little about hotels and staying in them...we just had not had the chance to do so...or the funds to make these types of plans. In the late sixties a Marriot Motor Inn opened on City Line Ave. in Bala Cynwyd. The hotel had two restaurants in it. One was a coffee shop and the scene of many lunches out when we might have gone shopping in Bala Cynwyd at Lord and Taylor. The other restaurant was the "fancy and exotic one"...the Kona Kai a Polynesian restaurant. It was owned by the same chain as had owned the "Pub" in New Jersey. The restaurant really played on the theme of Polynesia...a place that we knew nothing about at all...with servers in grass skirts, huts, and Tiki lamps lighting your way to your seat. In the background there was "hula" music playing to transport you to this exotic land. As a family we would go there for "special" occasions and share the "PuPu" platter, enjoying every bite of the choices that were offered...spareribs, shrimp, egg rolls...and a little barbecue in the middle to keep your food warm. Drinks were brought to the table in an artificial coconut shell and adorned with a colorful paper umbrella. When we went there it was like escaping to a land that was otherwise unknown and unattainable...and I must say that I have no memory of any unpleasantness occurring for the Hess family at the Kona Kai. It was so good to escape and have fantasies here with my family.

So I take you to the Marriot...a place of fond memories. During the Spring of 1972, it is not my family that is present there, it is the unsavory despicable men who were responsible for Martin's murder. Martin had testified for the government. He had cooperated and provided information in exchange for a promise that his sentence would be reduced or dismissed. I suppose word got back to the perpetrators that he had become a "stooly"... a snitch... and thus the plan needed to be put into place to silence him permanently. From court documents, "United States of America vs. Louis Martin Agnes, Anthony DiPasquale, Police Lt. Joseph Marker, Frederick Schiavo, Raymond Trainor," I learn the Grand Jury charges:

From on or about February 1972, up to and including August 7,1972 the defendants and co-conspirators and other persons known and unknown to the Grand Jury, did knowingly and intentionally combine, conspire, confederate and agree together, with each other and with other persons to commit certain offenses against the United States. It was the plan and purpose of said conspiracy to corruptly and by threats and force, endeavor to influence, intimidate and impede Martin Alan Hess, a witness in a court of the United States.

It was further the plan and purpose of said conspiracy to injure, that is, to murder, said witness, Martin Alan Hess, in his person on account of his testifying to matters pending in the Eastern District of Pennsylvania.

On or about March 1972, in the Eastern District of Pennsylvania, at the Marriot Motor Inn, the defendants and co-conspirators herein, Louis Martin Agnes, Anthony DiPasquale, Raymond Trainor, Joseph Marker and others did meet and did discuss means of murdering witness Martin Alan Hess. At the aforesaid meeting, defendant and co-conspirator Louis Martin Agnes did display a handgun equipped with a silencer.

On or about July 1972 the defendants and co-conspirators Anthony DiPasquale and Joseph Marker did meet and discuss the means of murdering the witness, Martin Alan Hess, and did discuss financial arrangements for said murder.

From this point on... multiple meetings and calls took place to work out all the last-minute details of my brother's murder. Anthony Di Pasquale leased an apartment in my brother's Cherry Hill New Jersey building in the name of Anthony Pasquale.

The day that my daughter Julie was born...... the last time I spoke to my brother... August 1... Joseph Marker paid "other individuals" $1500. a sum which represented partial payment for the proposed murder of my brother.

On August 6... Anthony Di Pasquale talked to individuals and instructed them on how to get to the Tower of Windsor Apartment. Those people all met then at the Tower of Windsor on August 6th... in my brother's very building and finalized the plans for the murder of my brother.

By August 7... they possessed the material... the explosives that would be used to blow up my brother's car with him in it... and they placed these explosives in the car.

The Marriot Motor Inn... so exotic to innocent Fredi. It's hard to remember if that last Spring we went there for a meal. Maybe we were there escaping reality, savoring every bite of that PuPu platter... while far in the darkness in another hut sat the perpetrators, plotting a murder. Martin passed me the last spare rib, while those men ate their ribs with a sauce of evil intent.

So alone in the world, Martin faces the day: An imagining

AUGUST 7, 1972.

"I'm shaving and getting ready to go to court today to testify... I see my face in the bathroom mirror and say to myself... well you are really all alone in the world today...

From every side I have been abandoned... no support from anyone... I suppose that this too is my punishment for thinking I was smart enough to play with the big boys and get out unscathed...

All of those damn criminals I have thought were my friends... not a one of them could be trusted... somehow all of them know how to protect their own asses and left me out to dry by myself...

After I testify today in court against some of them... I have no idea how I will spend the rest of the day... oh yeah I do have one customer to see so I suppose I will go to see the customer... and then what??? Who even wants to be in my presence anymore?... I have become trouble to everyone...

Friends... those the government has turned them against me... used them to frame me...

My family... they have been of no help to me either... they love me but they don't like me or approve of anything about me... they really have never understood me or what I needed in life... so it has been impossible to really ask them to support me in this situation... they are like babes in the woods. Yes, it was them who wanted me to do this testimony today... "Be a mensch! Clear your name... help our government solve this case... and then start over" that's what they told me... that's what they wanted and so I am doing so... I have no idea what it will mean for me to start over... what can I do now... and where will I go? Those details I have not discussed with my family. I am going all alone today... they will not be with me.

My mother... the one who has always been my support is with my youngest sister, Fredi. She just gave birth to her first child... Fredi and her needs are so much easier for mother to deal with. I suppose I could have asked mother to come with me... but I would never want to humiliate her the way today would humiliate her... she deserves better... better for her to have joy with a new baby...... than sorrow from me... again.

My father he is of no use to me. The two of us never saw eye to eye at all. I guess I am too much like him for him to admit... both of us men who prefer to be "dealing" out on the street... I was always better at it than he was... but he never got into any trouble... He came to court with me in March and said he would vouch for the fact that I was not a flight risk... I suppose that is something... but he could not look at me at all... he found out about Joey and me at that trial and that was more than he could take. He and I have had little to say to each other since then... except..."Be a mensch... and finally! try to do the right thing.

My sisters... they inhabit a totally different world than I ever had. We were close as kids but life has caused us to diverge... We talk in pleasantries about nothing at all... I spoke to Fredi last week the day she had her daughter, Julie... I was happy for her but what could I say? They have no idea of what today might mean for me at all...

So alone in this world...

And Joey, my dear Joey, he and I have been together for five years. I have supported him and encouraged him in that time. He is cute and sweet and not so bright... so without me he would have been nowhere at all. He has been my one confidant over these years. He has known every stupid thing I have involved myself in and all of the players who I have been mixed up with... he has been my everything... and even his mother... I have embraced her too and cared for her... they became the family that I could talk to and I thought even knowing everything about me... they loved me and accepted me... in spite of all the mess I had gotten into... they loved and liked me... not like my own family. Or so I thought... until I discovered that the government had turned, even Joey, against me. The one I loved the most in this world could be manipulated against me... unthinkable.

And even so... we were together all weekend... but in my heart I know that, that love will never be the same... I can no longer trust him either.

So alone in the world...

OK... so get going already... looking again in the mirror. I am dressed for court... and I will be there on time... I will tell all... I have never been so terrified...

Don't forget to put the curtains into the trunk of the car that you will deliver later in the day after court to that customer...

Tomorrow will be a new day... and then I will have so many things to figure out... where I will go next in my life, I really have no idea... maybe I will even take a ride to see my sister and that new niece, Julie... ?

Today... I feel truly overwhelmed by how alone I have become in this world......

Off I go......"

And so, on that last morning, after Martin put some merchandise into the trunk of the El Dorado, he went around the front and got in. When the engine started the bomb blew up the car with Martin in it. The image, the clothes, the cars the illicit activities all converged now to do him in, in this car... his life ended.

We always knew this day would come

MY BROTHER WAS always in some sort of trouble and I lived waiting for the day that it would destroy him. It was like he suffered from a terminal disease... his being... seeking out thrill... living on the edge... starting something with some good intention and then always taking it too far. Martin possessed fantastic creative energy that always had a way of becoming misguided. When would the "too far" finally catch up with him? That question was always in my mind and on some level... I knew for sure it would.

It was Monday August 7, 1972. My parents and in- laws and one of my best friends had all been with Heshie, Julie and I for the weekend. Everyone went home to Philadelphia late on Sunday... except my mother. She was going to spend the week with us to help me adjust to being a mother. She and I spent a wonderful and serene morning with Julie... bathing, dressing and feeding her... my mom (the nurse) instructing me all of the way. We finally tucked her in for a midday nap in her lovely new room... furnished with all new furniture... and a yellow shag rug that my brother had made. My mother suggested that I go to take a nap while Julie was sleeping... and she retired to the kitchen... a favorite spot for both my mother and me. So much excitement... a new mother... constant visitors and phone calls... a new city... a new residency for my husband... I was truly exhausted and in need of this nap.

My mother had purchased the ingredients to make spaghetti and meatballs for Heshie and me for Monday night dinner. It was a favorite for both of us, and my mother's comfort food. Her spaghetti was delicious and rich and the spicy comforting odor, a mix of tomatoes, garlic and oregano... was already lulling me into a much needed nap. Mother when in her "cooking zone" humming constantly to herself..."Begin the Beguine"... she had created a lullaby for me... and just as my eyes fluttered shut... I heard the door of our apartment open... and my husband Heshie(not even stopping to acknowledge my mother)... rushed in past my mother in the kitchen... and into our bedroom.

I was baffled...what was he doing home in the middle of the day? He had just begun his residency in pathology at Johns Hopkins Hospital... and it was not like him to come home like this. He did not approach me and his face was ashen. He stood remotely in a corner in our bedroom... and the look on his face gave me my answer. The day had finally arrived... He did not have to utter a word. I did it for him... I said: "he is dead isn't he?" and he just shook his head in reply. I knew that this was the day that Martin was to testify in a trial providing evidence against a member of the crime family that he had become a part of. He was to go alone to the trial... after all my mother was with me... and most likely my father could not deal with this or anything related to him, at all. The testimony was not to be, of course. The mob members assured that he could not make it to the courthouse to provide evidence against them. Martin knew he was in peril to do this, yet he did so anyway, without the proper protection that had been offered to him and that he allegedly refused. How was it possible that the Department of Justice allowed a naïve witness to determine on his own that he did not need their protection? Was his life so easily expendable to them? None of us really could understand what he was to do that day and how much danger he was in. It was now up to me to quietly enter my mother's domain... the kitchen and tell her that her first- born child... the one she had confided to me needed her to love him the most... had been killed that morning.

It was the most tragic day of my young and sheltered life. My mother too... looked at me knowingly as soon as I came into the kitchen... it was over... the day we had all dreaded had arrived. My mother and I screamed and wept together and waited for the rest of the family to arrive now... and take her home for her son's funeral. I went into Julie's room and looked at her peacefully sleeping and felt confused. I was sure that my mother had also looked at Martin on day six of his life and saw the perfect and beautiful little boy that she had brought into this world... and viewed him with amazement... the same amazement I felt whenever I saw or touched Julie. How could it be possible that it could all go so wrong in a life that was so innocent and precious?

On my first visit home to Philadelphia after Martin's death I came across a trove of clippings about my brother's death and the aftermath in my parent's apartment... and my mother "caught" me looking at them... she grabbed my hand and tore them from me... and angrily said: "don't ever take them out again... and do not ask me about them!" She frightened me... my mother was generally quiet and sweet and gentle with me. That was our relationship... and I wanted to keep it that way. So I took in her words and I vowed to myself never to make that mistake again.

This I suppose answers my question to myself: "Why were you content for so long to have so little knowledge about Martin's death and his life preceding it that brought all of us to that day?" I loved my parents more than I could even say... and I wanted to do what I thought they asked for in those painful days. So I went along...

Now I read: "Car Blast in Jersey Kills 'Star Witness and Key Mob Player' in a Narcotics Case." (NYT)

PART V

A Vow of Silence

Greetings from SUGAR BUSH MOTOR COURT,
BURKS FALLS, ONTARIO

Dear Fredi 9-6-60
How are you. Still going strong have had so far the time of my life. We Have stayed with some people for 3 days and learned alot. Love. Martin

CP 26
CANADA'S "PRIDE" - The Royal Canadian Mounted Police
Made in U. S. A.

Pub. by Canadian Post Card Co., Ltd., Toronto 3

POST CARD

Miss Fredi Hess
1119 E. Barringer St
PHILA. PA.
U. S. A.

Who he was to me

Jo Ann

TO THIS DAY, *I am struck by my own inadequacy in understanding the scene that unfolded in my own living room one week after Martin's death. My life was in turmoil. When my parents returned from Baltimore the week after Martin's murder, they arrived at my home with a planned meeting with Joey Conti, my brother's paramour. I had no knowledge of this prearranged meeting. I merely believed they came over to visit with me and my sons; and, to see how I was doing a week after the incident. I was wrong.*

When Joey showed up at my house, my mother embraced Joey and cradled him like a baby. While she rocked him in her arms sitting on a loveseat; my father moved to the other side of the living room... distancing himself physically. This was painful to witness. I went over to my father and placed my head in his lap and shared our sorrow weeping together. To this day, I cannot get the vision of my mother's embrace of Joey out of my soul. In retrospect I understand that my mother needed to touch the last human being who had embraced her son.

What's more disturbing about this recollection is that Fredi's extensive investigation of court records revealed that it was Joey Conti who turned state's evidence and shared information that eventually led to Martin's demise. He was the character who conveyed all pertinent information to the government. He knew about all of Martin's endeavors and whereabouts and shared them with the investigators. When it became evident that Martin's inactions with organized crime could possibly jeopardize the lives of others... his murder was inevitable. He had to be silenced.

I am certain my mother did not realize Joey's involvement at the time. Rather she just wanted to touch the person he loved. Regardless of the reality, that scene drove a wedge in my relationship with my mother that lasted for years. I strongly believed she didn't recognize the pain that caused me and how the tragedy impacted my life. One can only guess at a backward glance through the looking glass.

Recently a psychologist informed me that anyone who identifies as "gay" and who has heterosexual experiences is rightfully "gay." I believe that's probably true for Martin. Nothing would have been more reprehensible to our "macho" father than to recognize and accept a homosexual son. In those days, homosexuality was definitely considered to be aberrant behavior. I am not certain daddy ever came to terms with Martin's sexuality.

The picture of mother's clutching onto Joey Conti after his death remains a wound in my soul. Although I can accept her need to hold and touch Joey as the last human being who embraced Martin, I will never get over her need to mother him when her own children sorely needed her support.

As a mother, I can appreciate the need to hold close to people and things of a deceased family member. As a sibling to that member, my needs became circumspect... secondary... not recognized.

It is almost impossible to align my mature feelings with those of my mother in mourning. It took many years to get over my feeling alone and abandoned in my time of need. Because neither parent subscribed to nor believed in psychotherapy, I was never able to recommend it. I tried unsuccessfully to include mom in several sessions with my therapist hoping that she would come to recognize how much I was hurting and, how much I needed her support. Her unwillingness to engage made these sessions futile.

"Bereavement is ragged. Death is the most private and personal human acts: the ways we talk about death or grief or the silence that follows is a complex process. For someone writing about their own grief, there are no guidelines. The death of a loved one is also the death of a private, whole, personal and unique culture, with its own special language and its own secret, and it will never be again, nor will there be another like it."... writes David Grossman in "Falling Out of Time" about the death of his son.

It was a bang... an explosion, not a whimper that resounded from that day forward... forever until the respondent silence became deafening. There is a price for living in silence. The pain that each of us felt was introspective... that is... kept to ourselves. There was no place for discussion.

I am searching my memory for a time we shared our feelings of loss by phone or in person following his death. I find we didn't. It was as if there was an unwritten law that we didn't talk about it. It was too painful. I know Fredi and I shared our concerns about our parents but I can't recollect sharing personal stress and strain.

Sitting at Shiva for a 2nd cousin, I am reminded of other family tragedies and scandals. There were several unexpected suicides on both Mother's and Dad's sides of the family. I can recall the "noise" of each: shock and dismay accompanied by the absence of any discussion as to the "why."

With remorse, I regret that so many years went by with no discussion or conversation about what we had all lost. Even attempts at shared therapy never resulted or revealed shared unresolved, unexplained suffering. It was as if we didn't talk about it to each other or to a therapist... it didn't happen. But it did! And my defense of not wishing to revisit it was more about questioning purpose. Why? What could possibly be gained?!

In her study of writers' deaths, Katie Roiphe writes that "moving on, as a concept, is for stupid people, because any sensible person knows grief is a long-term project."

Routines, mundane daily, weekly and monthly events afforded our parents outlets that could divert their inner turmoil. I am sure they shared private periods of extreme anguish and mourning, but they never shared them with me. At all costs, those emotions were hidden and the fortress they build around it was never to be broached.

In retrospect, my failure to try to break through this wall was self-defense.

Anna Quindlen shares: "grief remains one of the few things that has the power to silence us." The truth is that we have lived with that silence for 45 years. Loss is forever: decades after the event there are occasions when something in you cries out of the presence of absence. In truth, I have put so much behind me that when I struggle to remember I cannot fathom where he was for my children's birthdays, bar mitzvahs, graduations or marriages. He was never there! He could not be a witness to life cycle events that were integral to my life. I resent this.

Fredi: Fulfilling birth-order roles: The baby stayed home

I WAS EXPECTED to be the sweet, easy, baby, if I could not have any attention it was fine with me as some of the attention that I saw my brother getting was negative and frightening. I was content to keep to myself and rarely even provide an opinion at the family table as my father was dogmatic and if he disagreed with any of us he would show his wrath quite easily.

This role of "family baby" came roaring to the fore on the day my brother was murdered. When the news came I had to fully rise to the occasion and help my mother in the first hours of this tragedy until the rest of the family assembled in our apartment in Baltimore. I was the "adult" child who cared for her in these first moments... but as the others arrived... I was again consigned to my role... as the sweet, innocent and vulnerable "little one."

As the information about the funeral was discussed I was told: "You cannot attend the funeral it would be dangerous for you having just given birth." When I asked what exactly that meant... I was told that such a traumatic exposure in one who had just given birth could possibly sink me into a deep post-partum depression. I asserted that this sounded like nonsense... but I was told if you don't believe us (my sister, my mother's sister, my father)... call your obstetrician and see what he says.

So I did. I called Dr. Neil Rosenshine immediately and explained the situation to him. He expressed his condolences and then told me that what my family had told me was correct... and that it was his medical opinion that I not attend the funeral. I accepted him at his word... after all he was the expert. It never occurred to me that I could refuse his counsel or my family's thoughts.

So when it was time to leave for Philadelphia for the funeral... my husband, my mother, my father and all went together. My aunt Shirley stayed with me and Julie. She and I spent the day of the funeral together trying both of us to know the right thing to do with my baby. By nightfall, Heshie and my parents returned to our apartment in Baltimore. Shirley and I had prepared a dinner and we all sat stone silent through that dinner. After dinner, Heshie took Shirley to a hotel where she remained until the weekend, joining us for a portion of each day.

I was "too fragile" to attend the funeral... but now I had my broken parents living with me in my apartment for the next eight days. Both of them were heavily medicated just to make it through the day and to be able to sleep. I have vivid memories of sitting at my kitchen table in the morning with my parents... after getting Julie fed and in for a nap. My father threatened daily to go out on the balcony of my apartment and jump... he had lost the will to live. I pleaded with him daily... Daddy please... I have lost my brother... I need you and mother in my life now more than ever! I seemed to be able to talk him off the ledge every day... but there was literally no room for me to grieve or shed a tear. When Heshie and I would finally get into a folding bed in Julie's room each night (my parents had taken our bedroom) I would quietly cry in his arms. This time of new life and joy so laden with fear and intense grief. I knew that each morning I needed to be "on" for my parents. I needed to try to help them just make it through another day. So the "baby"... the innocent, sweet... maybe not the brightest one in the family... had to bring tremendous strength and resilience to them... so that we all would survive. My parents could not sit shiva for my brother... and so we did not. Shiva was the daily routine of just existing for them... and this they did in my home... and in my embrace. We were alone... we did not have visitors or even phone calls to express condolences. Shame prevented others from knowing how to support us.

Several weeks later when I went for my first post-natal appointment with Dr. Rosenshine... I told him that I actually was doing fine psychologically... though I was very sad and grieving. I shared with him that I thought that I was experiencing what I should be experiencing having just given birth... and at the same time suffering the most significant loss in my life. He then confessed to me that against his better judgement... he had gone along with a request from the family to advise me that it would not be medically sound for me to attend the funeral. He regretted that he agreed to do so... but he did not really know me very well when this all had transpired as I only became his patient weeks before Julie's birth. He went along with the family's request as not to compound an already very difficult situation. He confirmed for me that sitting in front of him was a very strong new mother... who was handling both the new task of mothering and the intense grief very well. I was not surprised to hear his admission. I suspected that my family had done so in an effort to "protect" the "sweet, gentle... vulnerable baby of the family" from this difficult reality but I have never really recovered from this particular "family exclusion." I was robbed of the chance to really know that my brother was gone. In my heart, I forgave the doctor for this deception... as I think I understood the position he had been placed in. I never forgave our family rabbi... Maxwell Farber who presided at Martins' funeral. The rabbi had been "my rabbi" for all of the important milestones in my life... my Bat Mitzvah, my Confirmation, my wedding... yet, he too was complicit in the fact that I remained in Baltimore during Martin's funeral. He could not seem to pastor my family about what was the way to face death... fully. He never even called me to offer his sympathy or his joy at hearing of my daughter's birth. His shortcoming in this most crucial time in my life... was just one piece of my ultimate desire to become a rabbi. From him... on this occasion... I learned what a rabbi should not be!

Jewish tradition of death: not this time

I AM A rabbi now and as a pastor I value the manner in which the "rabbis of old" have laid out an entire system of law concerning the ways to accompany the dead to their final resting place and the way the family is to observe mourning. Even in Biblical texts there is a proscribed way to mourn the death of a loved one. In Biblical stories we learn that those who grieve their loved ones are expected to respond with sadness, putting ashes on their heads or tearing their clothes. They are to inflict obvious pain on themselves in reaction to the death of a loved one. Sadness not anger is what is proscribed.

I respect the rabbinic sages because I believe they grasped the psychological needs of the mourner and found the manner to help the mourner to grasp their loss and then to return to the business of living... all in the proper time.

As a rabbi recollecting my brother's death I am now even more dismayed with how we as a family dealt with it. His loss was shocking... and for all of us there was shame involved in "who he had become" and the manner in which he died. But I ask myself today did this shame earn him also a shameful end? Were we consigned to feel only anger at him for his death and not allow the customs to have us experiencing sadness? What would have been different, or even better for all of us if we had observed the law of the ancient rabbis? I feel had we honored him with all of the proper practices we could have rehabilitated him for ourselves. After all, in spite of all he had done and was done to him. we his family still loved Martin.

Shame forced us to follow a script that only acknowledged his misdeeds... we buried him and then we "were through with him and all of his evil." I feel such shame today that this transpired.

When my brother died my father had to go to the morgue and identify his body. Once he was there with his son and saw it was in fact Martin, his first born, what was in my father's mind, besides horror and grief?

My father was the religious "authority" for all of our family. He had been brought up ultra -Orthodox and so he alleged to know "all of the right things to do in any situation." Other members of the family would call my father to ask what was the proper thing to do in every situation.

So what do the rabbis say about what is to happen at the time of death? When the body is taken away to the funeral parlor the body is supposed to be guarded by religious men (today women in liberal Judaism also perform this duty) throughout the time that precedes burial. These guards recite Psalms over the body to assure its safety. Additionally, the body is bathed and prepared for burial in a formulaic manner also ensuring the "purity of every soul." My father knew this practice, I doubt he requested that it be followed for Martin. On reflection now I know he did not... how do I know?

The rabbis taught that each soul to be returned in its purity after washing is clothed in a pure white linen shroud, that makes each human equal at death before the almighty.

But I have a newspaper article showing his partner, Joey Conti leaving their apartment carrying one of my brother's shiny, silk "gangster suits," glitzy shoes, and gaudy tie for his burial. Joey brought all of this to the funeral director. My brother was buried as the "gangster" he had become.

Following burial the family is to return to their home and allow the community to surround them in their loss. Additionally, daily, three times a day a special prayer is recited by the family members closest to the deceased to acknowledge their loss while still affirming their own attachment to life. The formal practice is known as "sitting shiva" where the family is to sit for seven days in their homes and live in the reality that life is now to go on without this loved person as a part of it.

This never happened, shame cancelled this one too. My parents escaped to me in Baltimore. The community did not call or come. No one brought the "meals of consolation." No prayers were said. The mourners had no mechanism for "working through" the grief.

The first Shabbat after Martin's death my parents and I went to a synagogue in Baltimore on Friday evening to say Kaddish... the memorial prayer for him, for the first time. I am sure that this was the only time I said Kaddish for Martin with my parents. We were anonymous in this setting, no one there knew us or my brother and so they could not know the circumstances of his death.

The next morning, my husband, my father and my uncle went to a local Orthodox synagogue and named my daughter Julie at the Torah. I suppose my father also said Kaddish then. The women stayed home with the new baby. The pain and the joy were intertwined over one Shabbat.

We just put our heads down and tried to find a way back to life without the spiritual help... that we all had alleged to believe in.

When it was over, it was just over. We allowed ourselves to be consumed with silent anger at him. We had no means of accessing grief or sadness at his loss. There was almost no way to understand that he would never return to be a part of our lives that stretched out openly before all of us.

Martin's soul was not accompanied to a place of peace with the proscribed tradition. Was this God's plan for him... for us... that he should matter so little to not even warrant following tradition?

Tradition helps the mourner to properly stay in relationship with the one who is lost. Without tradition we were all robbed yet one more time.

Alone at last with Julie

A NEW BABY... BROKEN parents... my head spinning with all that I had to do to keep all of those inhabiting my apartment alive, fed, safe... and quiet. After eight days of this quiet my parents felt it was time to return home... to try to live in the presence of the ongoing press coverage of Martin's murder. They would remain home just a few days as we began a routine of their visiting every weekend, when it was possible to be bathed in the quiet of another city and of a new baby. The baby, Julie, offering all of us hope that the future could be redemptive.

And so I greeted that Wednesday morning... with resolve that she and I would finally get to know each other... and that she would gently comfort me in this upside down time. I would cuddle her to my chest and cry the tears that would not come until then... she would look deeply at me and assure me that together we would be alright. That was Julie at two weeks, that was Julie... in her very essence.

Her room helped to set this stage for comfort. The walls were bathed in a sweet yellow color and the curtains on the window and the yellow shag carpet on the floor completed the swath of light.

Julie and I sat peacefully on the brand new bentwood rocking chair in this haven, Martin had created for us. As I rocked, I whispered to Julie what had happened in the week that had passed... I wept and clutched her to me... and I breathed more deeply than I had in weeks. I told her:... Julie... the world we create for you will be so different than it was for Martin... I will make sure that I keep you safe, always. I repeated it over and over as the chair rocked slowly back and forth, trancelike. Just then, the phone rang and jolted me from this peaceful trance.

"Hello, Fredi it's mother (my mother-in-law, that is). We are surprising you. Dad and I are already on Route One and we are on our way to your house. We will be there in about an hour. We are staying over with you tonight. Make sure there is food in the apartment for lunch and dinner as we want to spend every minute we can with Julie."

What could I say? They were already on the way. I felt like I wanted to rip every hair out of my head. I wanted to be alone with my new daughter and with my husband. We so needed several days of peace and quiet together to get to know this new little lady… and we needed to figure out what it meant now to be parents. And I… I needed quiet to understand that my brother was dead and that my parents would never be the same parents I had had ever again.

But no, they were on their way, and they wanted lunch and dinner too! Fortunately the freezer had been stocked ahead for the birth of a new child… and while my parents stayed with me, I shopped and cooked for a chance to clear my head each day. I would escape to the market. My mother would escape to caring for Julie. It had helped all of us to get through that first week.

I dialed the phone frantically…" Heshie, your mother and father are on their way to Baltimore as we speak. They will be here in an hour and they are staying over. What could I say to them? They did not ask they told me… but I really need some peace and quiet right now!"

"Oh no"… Heshie exclaimed. I know this is horrible for you and I will try to come home from the hospital as soon as possible but you know I have missed so much time in the last two weeks… I too need to return to some normal routine… I am a brand new resident, after all."

Yes he was 100 percent correct. He would not be able to help me out until dinner time. They would be all mine in less than an hour.

This would be the only "visit of consolation" that I was to receive after Martin's death, I told myself. They were coming to pay their respects to me, that made sense.

Those fifty minutes flew by and the doorbell was already ringing. Julie was fast asleep and satiated. She was the picture of peace and quiet.

They stood at the door awkwardly. Celia, my mother in law… burst in, big as life. Nathan my father-in-law was silent, as usual. They came empty- handed except for their overnight bag.

"Where is she?," Big- haired blond Celia bellowed. We came to see her… not you!

Nathan shot me a knowing glance allowing that this was an inappropriate greeting for a daughter in law who had just had a death in her family. But that was Nathan. He was no match for Celia. He just let her be, and he stood in stoic silence.

"Mom, I offered, she is sound asleep. She just finished her bottle and she is generally out for several hours once she is fed."

"Well then let's have lunch we are hungry," Celia suggested.

And so, we sat down in the dining area and I brought out lunch. The dining area was also touched by my brother's decorating handiwork. He had covered the chairs in new fabric, a nubby yellow linen and made the round yellow shag rug for this room before we moved to Baltimore. I felt his presence as I awaited some words of comfort from my husband's parents.

Those words would not be forthcoming. Instead, Celia launched herself into a diatribe against me.

"How could you do this to us? We are such a good family. You know, your husband Heshie… he is everything that we ever dreamed of in life. He is brilliant and we always wanted our son to be a doctor and he has fulfilled that… although he is a resident in a field that we would not have chosen for him… that's probably your influence too. These past few months have been a nightmare for us. Your brother being caught working with the mob… it was all over the papers. You even allowed him into our house when we had a party when Heshie graduated from medical school…we asked you not to include him! But no…you did not listen. You let that gangster into our house! And then we were finally so happy about our first grandchild and then what? Your brother gets murdered… and it's all over the papers and on TV… it's the most humiliating thing we have ever experienced. You tricked our son and you tricked us into thinking you were such a fine young woman. Now we know the truth…you come from a terrible background and you now have all of us trapped… my son, my granddaughter… and us. We wish he could have a wife that came without all of that terrible baggage. What a mess you have brought into our lives!"

I was speechless... how was it possible that these words were rushing toward me?

Nathan said nothing at all... not a word to stop her... his eyes would not connect with mine. He heard how awful these words were... and I suppose he was used to it. He acted as defenseless as I was.

I just prayed that Julie would stir... that she would wake up and save me from this horror. I steeled myself... waited on the "queen mother"... and barely touched a morsel of the lunch myself.

"Just one more day" I said to myself in silence... just one more day of this abuse... then I can return to the comfort of my child... and my husband.

Julie's little cries finally rescued me from the onslaught. The grandparents and I went to her. I allowed big Celia to diaper her and feed her, her bottle. She was why they had come... and of course also to warn me... that I better not "mess up their lives ever again."

I escaped to the kitchen to begin those "dinner preparations"... tears streaming down my face. My life was making so little sense to me.

> A new apartment... in a strange city
> My husband starting a new residency...
> A new daughter... a beauty!!!
> My brother, murdered!
> My parents are broken and I must protect them!
> And now... my husband's family threatens me for what I have done?
> And I am told... you better be perfect... or else!

Ok, I will just lose myself in dinner preparations... and count the minutes until their son gets home. There are no words that I can speak to them. I am shaken to my core.

When they are gone... on the way back to Philadelphia I will try to understand the place I now stand. It will take many years of work on my part to reach Celia and I work mightily to do so.

Even my friends thought it best to be silent!

A FIRST CHILD... AND then a terrible tragedy... how were people able to respond to this set of issues?

They were unable and it sounds crazy but I did not have any expectation that they would. I felt in my bones that what had just happened to me was so out of the ordinary and so horrible that it was normal that my friends did not call, they did not come, they did not write me a note.

Even the joyous part, the birth of my first child was somehow now seen as too awkward to deal with... even though just the week before Martin's murder everyone was excited about Julie too. Once these two events converged it was impossible for anyone to know what to do.

Only one friend from Philadelphia called. My friends had moved into the apartment in Philadelphia that we vacated when we moved to Baltimore. Her call to me was also not really one of consolation.

Here was what it consisted of:

"Hi Fredi, just wanted to check in with you to ask you why you gave your brother permission to use your address as his address?"

"What are you talking about," I responded.

"Well in this morning's paper it reads that your brother had many different addresses where he said he resided and this one is listed as one of them. Why did you allow him to use this address after you left the apartment to us?"

"Permission... I answered... I never gave him permission to use that address and he never told me he was using it. I am totally shocked and so sorry that this has happened. I really don't know what to say about this at all!"

"Well as you can imagine we are quite unhappy about this as is our family as now we are living in this apartment and perhaps some of his enemies will target us where we live," she said.

"Again," I pleaded..."I knew nothing at all about him doing this and obviously I cannot now ask him as he is gone. I can only hope that nothing comes of the fact that he used this address. If there is anything that does happen please know that I will do whatever I can to rectify it."

"Well, that's all for today. I just had to check with you about this and see if you knew. I will let you know if any help is needed," she replied.

And then that was it. Another thing I was left with. Will any of our friends... some I had been friendly with my entire life still be my friends? Will this horrible event cause them to abandon me?

Somehow it never occurred to me to expect that they would reach out to me in friendship. All I felt was fear that I would lose this part of my life too, and fear to ever share with my friends what I was going through.

I did remain connected to those friends even though we lived now in different cities. We talked about the rhythm of our lives now that most of us had children and were no longer working. We were all trying to figure out whether motherhood would be the be all and end all for us. I had already found myself back in school in pursuit of a master's degree as I found that I needed my own fulfillment outside of the life of mother. In all of our interactions though, the topic of my loss was never mentioned.

They knew that my parents came to Baltimore weekly to visit and escape Philadelphia. No one ever asked how they were doing either... and I did not bring it up.

Forty-six years later, I am still connected to all of those same people and finally ask them why they never talked to me, called about Martin's death, sent food, visited, or even sent a baby gift after Julie was born.

I learn from them that they were too stymied to know what to do. Their own mothers advised that they should not broach this topic... unless... I did! They felt too embarrassed to ask me and hoped that if I wanted to talk that I would. They said they were too young then to know what to do about any death... and therefore even more so they did not know what to do about Martin's murder. They waited to see if I would say anything.

They did not know that I could not say anything. That this too felt so impossible for me. I wanted some normalcy in my life and I wanted my connections to remain intact. I suspected that if I had spoken to any of them of my loss they would run away from me very quickly.

I stayed safe. I spoke of life in Baltimore. I spoke of Julie and asked about their children. We exchanged recipes. We gave each other child rearing advice. We remained on the surface so that we could stay connected.

And so it remained that way for years.

The empty seat at the table

HE WAS NO more. And we continued.

It was so much quieter and it was so much more like the "norm" that somehow we all had always desired. We were now a family that did not have "the problem" in the center of every encounter that we had together.

Not even one year later... Pesach 1973... so in contrast to the horrific year before. The day we all knew what Martin was about... the day we could not turn our faces away thinking this too shall pass.

Pesach 1973... Spring has begun to make its presence known. The days were lighter and there were daffodils peaking up through the grass in front of my apartment building in Baltimore. This apartment has been the "starting over" point for Heshie, Julie and I... but also for my parents. It has been the light filled refuge from the continuing "bad news coverage" in Philadelphia.

Oddly, Baltimore was a simpler place to be... even if it had not been for Martin's death. It was at least fifteen years behind the times of life in Philadelphia. So there was an innocence, a simplicity, that colored all of our lives there. In the suburb in which we lived... life seemed idyllic. Here... Jewish people lived segregated from others in a community in which there was an entire street lined with synagogues. The stores in the shopping center reflected this segregation as well. The delicatessen and bakery were kosher. The card and gift store had cards, gifts and decorations for "our" holidays. At home in Philadelphia... life was once this way but had become more diverse. Somehow... this "Jewish concentration" was just what I needed to traverse this new time. It felt like I could travel back to my "old neighborhood" that had been that way and recapture those days...

that seemed less complicated... that seemed like we had been a "good Jewish family"... not one in which the first- born son... had gone so wrong. When my parents visited weekly they too seemed to relish this "simpler" Jewish ghetto of Pikesville... it was a new beginning in a simpler time.

Pesach, 1973...

We could not come home this year for the seders as Heshie's residency would not allow the time in Philadelphia. Another step for me, for us, in having our own "Jewish Home."

In the months in Baltimore I had created a Baltimore family that knew me only from the time that was centered in our lives as new parents. Most of this family were just like us... the men were all residents at one hospital or another... and the women were all just beginning to understand what it meant to be a mother to a first child. I invited all of our "Baltimore Family" to our seder that year.

It really represented a true departure from seder 1972... I would be with an artificial family... and this one did not have "Martin and his problem" present at the table.

When I decided to make the seder, I consulted my mother about the recipes I would need to make the meal totally traditional and tasting like she had prepared all of the foods. Mother wrote all of her recipes for me in her beautiful... artistic hand and mailed them to me in plenty of time for all that I would need to do. She sent me the recipes for: Gefilte Fish, Matzoh Farfel kugel, Sponge Cake, Potato Blintzes, and Lemon Sherbet... these were all my favorites for Pesach. Mother signed the letter: "I love that you are carrying forward my traditions, my daughter. I hope the cooking goes well... of course we can discuss all of this as you need to. Love and kisses, Mother."

Normalcy... that's what this seemed to indicate for all of us. We had left that terrible year behind.

When it was time to cook... mother talked me through every recipe. She loved that I was so much like her... that I so wanted to be like her... a good wife, a good mother... a good entertainer. In me, she could see the best version of her own story.

The seder table was lovely and everyone was so impressed with what I had been able to prepare. At this table all was full of life, fun and companionship.

Though tired from all of the preparation I felt that I was becoming my own "grown-up." I had prepared my first seder... and I had done it just as mother would have.

In her words and instructions Mother seemed just like "mother had always been to me." Sweet, kind and supportive... and seemingly now "unburdened" by the "trouble" that had always been in the background. To this day, when I prepare my seder meals those yellowed, stained and precious pages still come out and show me yet again how to "be like my mother." I use them... tears streaming down my face... she is with me as I continue to prepare her delicacies. That first year after... I now ask myself... how could you have been so ready for me to require you Mother... to just cheerfully help me to make my first seder? It has taken an entire adult life to comprehend how difficult that really was.

And I tried to start out all over again... in a totally new way.

- At my own table
- With my young husband and perfect daughter
- With a family of "colleagues"
- With my mother's recipes... familiar scents wafting through my kitchen
- Feeling I had my mother back again in a familiar way (for the moment)

Just the fact I had found that I could have a holiday and not miss him. I could have my mother's help and guidance again without "hearing the pain" in her voice...

In my Baltimore refuge... life could go on without him at my table.

What a simplistic way of understanding life.

And even two years later it is still news

"Jailhouse Lawyer Agnes Impresses the Judge."
—Evening Bulletin May 6, 1975

ALMOST THREE YEARS after my brother's death the newspapers continued to reference it as they covered the bad actors who were involved and who continued to be involved in a life of crime.

Agnes in particular was "supposed" to be the ringleader in organizing and planning the "hit" on my brother. What was clear as day was that Agnes knew the system in and out and therefore knew how to work it well enough that he often did not bear responsibility for the crimes that he committed .He often got off or got a suspended sentence. In the above referenced article, the judge complemented Mr. Agnes on his pursuit of knowledge concerning the law. He had been granted permission to attend classes and leave the jail in order to do so. He had a role in prison as an advocate for the prisoners that were his colleagues. The judge was adequately impressed with Agnes and his studies and the service that he was providing that he offered: "I don't want to preclude you from doing what you have been doing." Ultimately in this trial he did get sentenced to jail time-- what was he being tried for this time? He was tried for seeking to influence two jurors in the murder trial that was connected to my brother's death. In the original murder trial Mr. Agnes was acquitted.

But how had that happened? How had he and most of the other players gotten off in that trial? The jury, it was later proven," had been tampered with." Evidence showed that Agnes perhaps had paid as much at $100,000 to assure that the two jurors could be approached and bought off. A prisoner in jail at the same time that Agnes was (on another charge this time)... reported that Agnes had given him a list of the murder trial jury and checked off the two names of jurors who should be approached. The two, it was reported were unemployed and should be anxious to get their hands on some real money. This prisoner worked with someone out on the street to contact these two jurors. The friend initially went along with the plan and attempted contact but gave up when he became fearful of consequences. Ultimately, the prisoner aware of this scheme wrote a letter to the Camden County prosecutor to report all of the efforts to contact the jurors.

In the end only one of the seven men tried for my brother's murder did any time at all. The rest of the defendants were let go as the jury "could not reach a verdict." There would never be justice in this case. My brother's murder would just go unpunished.

And Louis Agnes, for years after, continued in a life of crime and subsequent stints in jail... for buying off the jury in my brother's murder... racketeering, counterfeiting... on and on... but he knew the system and somehow how to get the minimum sentence each time.

Ample evidence of the plot to murder my brother existed. Most of it was directly tied back to Mr. Agnes. But this "jailhouse lawyer" knew how to work it all to be acquitted, in the face of all the signs that it was him .all along.

Leviticus 16

"After the death of the two sons of Aaron..." —Leviticus 16:1

IT IS THE reading that is included for the holiest day of the year, Yom Kippur. We read in this portion about the role of ritual and of doing things in a proscribed manner.

What happened to Aaron's sons that caused their death? They did something wrong... they sinned... they came too close to God, and they did so in an improper fashion. On Yom Kippur morning we begin with this reading to invite us to understand that we must follow ritual in a proper fashion... if we ignore this... and sin, then we too could lose our lives like Aaron's sons, Nadav and Abihu.

The text also speaks of how Aaron dealt with the death of his two sons. He did so with utter silence, not a word was uttered.

These two sons having done something wrong, were not to be spoken of again. Their deaths were to remain in silence. Aaron was not to share his heartbreak, there would be no acknowledgement of their passing... no community response to their leader and his unfathomable loss. There was just silence...

Even in our most ancient text, the text that we read and reread every year there was some understanding of my family and the response to the death of my brother.

Like Nadav and Abihu, my brother did not follow what was expected. He drew too close to dangerous fire... and the danger... the lack of normal ritual caused him to lose his life.

Unlike, Nadav and Abihu, my brother was not a zealot for religion or God... but he was a zealot for the forbidden. If it was forbidden it invited him to "draw near to it"...

In both cases we learn that "drawing near" to what has not been the ordinary response or ritual could have a deadly outcome.

Aaron... could not even utter a word on learning of his sons' deaths...

This too ringing loudly in my ears... my parents... they so like Aaron.

When death comes, out of order... and instantly and unexpectedly... and with shame for doing what was not ordained by society... there are no words...

Aaron sunk into silence, perhaps out of shame for what his sons had done. After all, they were the sons of the High Priest, they should have known better... and perhaps they did and then "drew near with strange fire" anyway. Aaron just left with deep pain, sorrow and shame.

My parents and all of us... we were so like Aaron. We were shocked, we were in pain, we were humiliated by the "improper acts" that Martin had been involved with... and so we too, were silent. There were no words that we could speak about this unusual death... and no words could be spoken to us to comfort us.

Like Aaron... silence... was the only answer.

Oh my, this silence has biblical origin... the Hess family did not invent it.

And like Nadav and Abihu... perhaps Martin had no longer been a sinner... he had tried to "do" the right thing...

But it was too late... he had drawn too close to danger... and in the end, only silence would suffice.

Mother: Before and after

MY MOTHER WAS in many ways my best friend. There was nothing that I ever kept from her. We talked together endlessly… about life, boys, clothes. And I loved spending time with her. The usual activities that we shared together were cooking, marketing, shopping and going to the beauty parlor. In each of these activities I felt warmth, caring and security.. My mother made me feel like I mattered and I was valued. She also made me feel that as much as I loved being with her she loved being with me.

When I began dating it was our habit for mother to "wait up for me." After the guy had left our house… mother would get out of bed and meet me in my bedroom. We would sit on my bed together and pick apart every aspect of the date… and every word said… and maybe even every kiss… and determine together what it meant. Would this guy be the "one"? Had he risen to that stature? Would he call me back for another date… and how quickly could I expect to get that call? On my bed in my room… I told her everything!

I am quite certain that I had witnessed this same closeness and intimacy between mother and Jo Ann… when Jo Ann had been at this same stage.

She wanted everything to be right for us… and all of the talking was our way of paving the way for it to be so.

She was sweet, calm, wise… she was all mine… she was my friend… she was my mother.

That was before.

After, my mother was permanently changed.

She still was central to my life. But now... the smile was so hard to elicit. She was using all of her energy to just live. What this looked like was that my mother dutifully and expertly did her job as a nurse. She remained a devoted wife to my father assuring always that he was well cared for and a central focus of her attention. My mother was the most devoted grandmother that any grandchild could wish for. She loved everything about her four grandchildren and was always present for them. What had changed was there was always a veil that I could detect and an underlying sadness that I had not known before. She showed me daily that her quiet strength was enabling her to be all of the above, even in the presence of an enduring sadness.

The depth of dialogue was greatly reduced as we now just scratched the surface.

I was always on my best behavior. My mother made me a bit nervous now. She was so different and I did not quite understand how to navigate this new phase of our life as mother and daughter.

All I could do now was observer her closely. How does she look today? How does she seem? How does her voice sound? If any of those questions were answered in the negative to myself... I worked to reverse how she was feeling with all of my might. I wanted to have my old mother back again and I tried to coax our conversation to the place that had been so easy and familiar to both of us.

I guess if I had pushed, or if I had touched it, it might have broken her heart for certain. She had built a protective shield around herself, quite effectively.

My job, now for the duration was to keep her heart intact, and so I did it. I never made her talk, reflect, relive any of the pain of the loss of her beloved son.

In truth, it would never ever be the same again. I was in some ways the mother now... at 24.

Searching for my dead brother

I WAS ROBBED of ever really mourning my brother in many ways:

- I was not permitted to attend his funeral
- The family did not observe shiva
- My parents saw themselves as the only mourners and discounted the impact that Martin's death had on Jo Ann or myself

All of this contributed to an odd disconnect from the reality of Martin's death.

Two years after his death I moved back to Philadelphia... and right into the same apartment complex that my parents lived in. I suppose that my need to protect and comfort them in their loss made it imperative for me to live as close to them as possible.

So when back in the neighborhood in which I grew up... with my family and my brother... I began to really have a sense that he was "gone" and was never coming back...

But again the "unreality" of this would sneak in...

I found myself in the supermarket doing my weekly shopping and feeling quite certain that the man that just walked in the door... was my brother. There were definitely those times when I needed to follow that person around the market... just to check that it was not him.

And of course... I could not repeat this to anyone... they might think I was crazy... but what if... he had really gone into witness protection... and was not dead... ?

What if he still existed somewhere and I could find him and talk with him about what had happened.

I understood very little that this "unreality" that I was experiencing was totally normal... and was felt by many siblings who lose a brother or sister. I was still searching for him, and searching to understand that he would be permanently absent from my life, from this point going forward. I wanted desperately to discuss this with my family... that we "all" had a deep and lasting loss that would shape us going forward... but there were no words to use to do this.

It took me about a year after I returned to truly grasp... that . Martin was gone... my childhood connection to him was now broken... and following "phantom" people around the market or the mall... was not going to alter this fact.

The message that everyone had given me was that my loss was not in the same category as my parent's loss had been and that I had better get over it already... " Pull yourself together"... and I was very good at this... at following messages transmitted to me. I always aimed to please.

So after all of these years... I search for real... not in the aisles of the supermarket... or the face that looks like an older version of Martin. I search in the recesses of my mind. I search through real records that recorded the ending of Martin's life and the aftermath. I search... I keep searching... and in all of this, I do find him.

I find both the brother I loved and the brother that was troubled. My search has found the real Martin... to me... to us... Martin.

But to others, "Marty"...

In finding him I have learned to recognize both Martin and Marty.

This is what this has been about all along.

Discovering an important piece of the puzzle

MEMORY CAN BE faulty, we but think we remember something so clearly and in vivid detail.

My memory: It was about a year after my brother died and I had come to Philadelphia with Julie to visit my parents at their apartment. I am not sure why this trip to Philly was one in which I chose to sleep at my parents small apartment...which meant for me on the sofa and Julie in their room...but that is what I remember.

On one particular afternoon during that visit I put Julie in for a nap while my mother was in the kitchen cooking dinner. During her nap I opened a closet in their bedroom and found a manila envelope that contained articles pertaining to my brother's death. I stealthily stood outside my parents' bedroom in the dressing alcove and perused them . My memory pictures a cover story article in the Philadelphia Magazine about my brother... and the machinations of how he became involved with the mob. Before I could finish reading and take in any details about it my mother's hand was on mine and she angrily took the articles from me and said... "Please never again go through my things and take these out." I was horrified that I was caught, and horrified that I had made my mother so angry. I quickly apologized and shook my head in affirmation that this would never happen again. What I was totally unable to say to her was: "I need to know about this, I need to understand it, I need to talk with you about it." No. I was like a statue, a mute statue who lost my voice and my ability to verbalize all of the pain and the lack of knowledge that I had about my brother, a brother that I loved. Dinner was a bit awkward that night with all of us aware that I had crossed a Rubicon that was not to be crossed.

I could not forget that article.

Forty five years later, I am on the eve of my 70th birthday and Jo Ann will be 74 in the Spring. The two "elderly" sisters have set out to the place that we are told the archive for the magazine exists, The Pennsylvania Historical Society. It is interesting that I have convinced my sister to be a part of this project as initially...when I shared it with her she wanted to maintain the family silence. Now we have both determined that we could do this work together... as we have shared so much of life to this time.

It is a beautiful Fall day...picture perfect, in fact... sunny with a cool breeze and it is Halloween(one of my brother's favorite holidays). The ride in town was replete with memories of our childhood and commentary about the trees and leaves... in the name of our parents who often marveled at the beauty of nature often as they drove together in the car.

The Historical Society could be a movie set for a research library. The tall windows, the walls lined with tomes of all sorts and the long wooden tables and library lamps gracing the room. All was silent there as we put in our request for the issues of the Philadelphia Magazines from Fall of 1972, all of 1973 and 1974. We felt quite certain that the article would be found in one of these issues. My sister let me take the lead in the request... as she saw herself as "along for the ride." We have learned throughout the years that there are often emotionally charged situations that I have to take the lead in... in spite of the fact that she is the "older" sister... and on the surface the more assertive one.

We divided up the volumes and then went on our search. Jo Ann finished each volume with greater rapidity than I did. We could not find the article! It made me sure that one of us had missed it somehow and so we exchanged volumes and checked the work of the other... no article found.

So what was this search about? Did both of us "misremember" the article that appeared in the magazine? While I had only briefly seen it Jo Ann even remembers reading it. Could it have actually appeared at a later date? We both doubted that as the story would then have been too old and of little interest to the reader by then.

We left the Historical society confused. We both know we had seen this article... and I also remember my parents cancelling their subscription... at some time after it appeared as they felt that it was a magazine that sensationalized everything (they were correct about this).

Two elderly sisters now united in our search for our past… and the way to articulate it with integrity. We are now grasping for what remains of Martin… there is so little that we have…we have just memory and some of it may be faulty.

Newsflash!!! The old sisters were not "misremembering"…

When recounting this search to a lifelong friend and my frustration… he assured me that he too remembered an article about Martin! Later, he went himself to the Main Branch of the Philadelphia Library and found a short article written in Martin's memory by the author, Gaeton Fonzi. The article was a beautiful. It showed me that another saw in my brother the parts that I most fondly cherish. Fonzi, reported that he could see in Martin… intelligence, sweetness, and his gentle eyes and thoughtful approach… mixed in with his knowledge of how far off course he had gotten and how desperate he had become. He wrote that my brother had asked this author to tell his story… and the author seemed to indicate at the end of the short piece that he would do just that.

First step into the family synagogue—after

MY PARENTS HAD avoided most of their friends and certainly the family synagogue in the days following my brother's death. The only time they had attended synagogue to say kaddish was with me that first Friday night after his death in Baltimore... in a place where they would not be recognized as the parents' of the murdered mobster... Martin Allan Hess.

In Jewish tradition the most intense mourning period comes to an end after thirty days... this is referred to as the "shloshim period... meaning 30 days. When this time comes some of the practices that indicated that the mourner is most removed from society begin to abate. So it was quite ironic that the 30 day period coincided that year with Rosh Hashanah.

I don't recall if there was ever any conversation about "just skipping" attending the family synagogue that year to avoid the difficulty of facing the entire community... and our rabbi. What I do know is that we did wind up going to Emanu-El our lifetime Jewish community for the holiday. This synagogue was the place of so much of our family story up until then. The list of family connections to it and milestones marked there was long and included each of the three Hess children:

- Consecration when each of us began religious school
- Bar and Bat Mitzvah
- Confirmation for all three children
- Two weddings... my sister's and my own
- Every holiday

- Weekly Shabbat
- USY for Jo Ann and Martin
- Synagogue dances
- Martin as synagogue youth director
- Family friends... and friends for the children

So much of our lives revolved around that synagogue.

Rosh Hashanah meant seat 3 and 4 in Row W, on the right side of the main synagogue, facing the cantor. My parents had reserved seats always in the same place and we sat there in a small community of the same people year after year. The Bermans who sat seat 1 and 2, the Braits in front of them... and I can now picture the other people on their row and in front and back of them... but cannot remember all the names. It was prestigious to sit in the main sanctuary... and it was always my brother who "snuck" us in without the needed "ticket."

So it would be painful for my parents, tortuous, to walk into that sanctuary and take their seats on row W. My parents would feel that "all eyes" were glued to them and their every move. But it was a first step on the stoic road that they chose to travel.

I, of course, saw my role as making that most painful road a tad less painful. My husband and I decided that we would "come home" for Rosh Hashanah this first year and bring the new baby for everyone at synagogue to see. Julie was the distraction already.

We arrived at the synagogue right on time... even with a month old baby. Julie was "dressed up" in a High Holiday outfit. My parents had saved two seats for us on their row... as one of the stalwarts was not attending that year... and everyone understood that my parents needed whatever was necessary to be able to just "be there" for the holiday.

There was fuss over Julie, and oohs and ahs and many wishes of Mazel Tov, as well. This was what made sense to all of those people who had known my parents for most of their married lives that they had spent in this synagogue. It was our place of celebration... it was not a place to bring such sadness and shame that our family had just experienced.

Baby Julie, in her little knitted pink dress was the center of attention. It worked. My parents were able to be in synagogue for Rosh Hashanah with us at their side.

After just thirty days, we had turned our faces already to life, and away from pain and horror.

Sheloshim, thirty days was completed, and we immersed ourselves in the book of Life and Blessing.

This year that we began would be for sweetness, life and blessing. We were so glad that the year we had finished had passed.. We had made it through that terrible event and now we could look ahead. We were not yet to comprehend that even in looking ahead it would travel with us consistently.

Thank you, President Richard Nixon!!

IN JUNE OF 1972 Nixon had directed the Watergate burglars to break into the Democratic office headquarters in Washington DC. Two months after this my brother was murdered.

In the aftermath of Martin's death, my parents traveled every Friday to Baltimore to stay with my husband, my new daughter and I for the weekend.

President Nixon traveled with them every week. It became our custom during those visits to spend Friday night glued to the TV watching the commentary about what had been discovered about the break in in the week that had just passed. So many years ago, news was something that you had to wait for, and we did. After the news update we would then spend our time discussing the meaning of the new developments in detail.

Nixon provided quite a backdrop all of us to forget our own personal pain and scandal. In a crazy kind of way... the ritual that we took on in watching and talking about Nixon... supplanted our need to "say kaddish" for Martin, or discuss what had happened to us. This was something compelling to distract us that everyone in our country was involved in studying, it was Nixon, the crooked president!

By the time we returned to Philadelphia the family had already lived through two years without Martin and a new daughter was on the way, one who would be named for Martin. And that summer, we had hours of TV to keep all of us busy as each day uncovered yet one more wrinkle about Nixon.

When Emily, Martin's namesake was just a month old, Nixon resigned as President of the United States. We had traveled through these most difficult years with him in our constant thoughts. He oddly helped to keep us away from personal pain, he allowed us to experience national pain, in its place.

Oddly... I believe Nixon also gave my parents a reason to live and a source of personal outrage that they could verbalize.

Thank you, Richard Nixon.

New life

I WENT INTO labor with Emily… daughter number two on the hottest day of that summer. It was a difficult labor and delivery… and the first night after her birth I also was quite ill. Emily was a beautiful blond- haired, blue eyed baby… quite a surprise to me to have a baby that looked so different from me… after having Julie… who resembled pictures of me as a baby. I was thrilled to have this "new life" with us in a new season… one that offered only hope after two very trying years.

The day after Emily was born my father came alone to the hospital to meet the new granddaughter. I was baffled about why my mother was not with him… but I took one look at his face and I knew that all was not well… again. He looked like he had when my brother died… deflated… wan… flat… and I saw that he was ill at ease in my presence. He stayed only a few minutes with no explanation about why he looked as he did… and why he had not brought my mother along with him.

As soon as he left me I called Jo Ann.

"Tell me, what was wrong with Daddy today? And why didn't mother come with him to meet the new baby?"

My sister let me know that while I labored to deliver Emily… the jury delivered also…

For the jury it was a verdict in the trial of several of the men who had plotted to kill my brother. And the jury had dismissed all charges in the case. It was as though we had just traveled right back to August 7, 1972. My parents were tossed again down into a deep sense of mourning.

A new Obstetrician found me crying uncontrollably when he came around on rounds... Ironically, he immediately thought he had a case of post-partum depression on his hands... but I asked him to close the door of my room and I told him all that had transpired in the past two years and why my tears were perfuse. He got it... and became the "pastor" helping me to face my parents the next day when they both came to meet Emily. Dr. Corson let me sob and rant and he sat rapt, deeply listening to the entire story. He never rushed me or made me feel he had more important patients that he needed to get to. He stayed as long as I needed him to stay, until I was able to lessen my sobs. He also gave me counsel. Not about anything medical. He spoke quietly about how best to greet my parents and speak with them. He offered me the strength that I needed to face this loss, yet once again in the midst of my joy. Yet again, a doctor was truly able to "see me" and offer the words that were needed more than any medicine.

When my parents came to meet my new daughter, three of us, my mother, my father and I, drank in her beautiful face. They were touched that she would be named for my brother: Martin Alan... Emily Anne.

The topic of the trial was not approached until several weeks later when my parents came to talk with Jo Ann and I about it. There was information in the news and the papers, that perhaps the jury had been "tampered with" and that is why the perpetrators had gotten off. My parents wanted to pursue this matter, as they could not accept that my brother's murder would not be avenged. Jo Ann and I understood, we held them and wept with them .We also pleaded with them.

"Martin will never be brought back to us... even if these people are tried again... he is gone... and we are terrified!"

Here we were, the mothers of four young children living in the same city as the men who had plotted to kill and did kill our brother. We all had seen what they were capable of if they were crossed, and we truly feared for all of our lives. We begged them not to pursue this matter further. We feared that nothing good could be the result of such a pursuit.

And then that was that... the case was closed. They agreed to do as we asked. From this request came the silence that would endure.

From our fear of forces that we could not understand... that we had few resources to address... came quiet... a quiet that would become a protective shield for all of us that remained.

In synagogue... my father, my husband and his father went to the Torah and named my daughter:

Emily Anne... Menucha Aviva... restful Spring...

This was how we could carry him forward... his death unavenged...

But acknowledged... Emily Anne.

And Emily's namesake Martin was still in the news even when she was close to a year old. In a trial for the police officer that was involved in Martin's murder the officer acknowledged:

"All three of us that knew Marty, Norman Felt, Paul Rubin and I formed a partnership with Louis Agnes, considered to be the big man in the drug trade. The three entered into a pact that if anyone informed on somebody else or on the group the informer would be dealt with. They interpreted that to mean anyone who informed would be killed."

So Emily Anne, your namesake made that major mistake in life. He informed on his partners and paid with his life. He was not "restful."

His name, and his legacy offered a chance for redemption as you carry it forward.

A small crack in the wall of silence

IT WAS THE Fall of 1996. Emily was about to move to Israel and would become an Israeli citizen. It was a time of high emotion for our family… a daughter starting her adult life in a foreign country… so far away… on her own… in a place that was often dangerous. My heart was bursting with pride that I had raised such an incredibly brave and visionary young woman. She was fully ready to take off on this new chapter of life… fluent in four languages and possessing surety about why she wanted to live her life in Israel. My heart was also torn apart… my child was my life and now there would be entire seasons of her life… and my own life that we would experience a world apart. We entered this new time… before cell-phones, internet and easy connection with so many mixed emotions.

The week before Emily left for Israel I had lunch with my mother and as we shared our feelings about this very significant life marker in my own life as a mother, my mother said:

"Did you know that we had looked into sending Martin to Israel after he had been arrested?"

How could I have known this… no one had ever talked to me about the trouble he had gotten into…

I shared my shock at this statement with my mother and carefully stated that there was so much that I did not know about that time at all, hoping we would finally now have an opening.

But the window only opened a crack.

Mother shared that my parents had spoken to someone about the possibility of sending Martin to Israel after he had been arrested. They wanted him to start his life over again in a new "world"–our homeland. She told me that they pursued this up to the point at which they learned that it was impossible to "just send him there" with an arrest on the books. Martin would be extradited right back to the US at customs. He could not escape the charges that he had been found guilty of, and just be whisked away in this fashion.

After sharing this with me, the window closed again.

That was all mother wanted me to know…just that Emily was going to live in the land that they wanted my brother to escape to. Emily had been raised to want this possibility for her life…we loved Israel and had made it a central part of our family's life… and my children's growing up experience…

Perhaps… that "witness protection program" could have sent him there… our other home… and he could have been safe.

I know well today that Israel is not a paradise free of trouble… it could have found him there too…

Martin the Israeli… that's the most mother ever was to share with me.

Ironic Addendum: Their idea to send Martin to Israel had not been so far-fetched after all. In doing my research I read carefully through a court docket sheet for one of my brother's arrests. In this case he was arrested with six other defendants… five of whom seemed also to be Jewish (in relation to their names). So again… this myth that if my brother was involved with the "mob" all of the folks that he was involved with would be Italian… My brother had gotten in trouble with both Jewish and Italian folks… and not all of them even men!

The docket listed as one defendant… Zena… another person I had never heard of in relation to my brother--.but she and most of the others had gotten off or gotten probation for their misdeeds, only Martin somehow was the "guilty one" who was going to have to do time. Zena it seemed worked out a deal… in March of 1974 (after Martin's death) that allowed her probation in this case to be suspended. What was the deal? The record showed that her probation was to be lifted as she was now going to reside and work in Israel.

Zena found the way out… she went "home"… I wonder how that all worked out for her?

The silence breaks

WHEN EMILY WAS two years old we joined my sister and many of my friends as members of Adath Jeshurun Congregation in Elkins Park, Penna.

It became our family synagogue and soon after we joined my parents and my mother-in-law joined us there. It was a central part of our lives, in particular, our Jewish lives.

My sister's husband's family was one of the founders of this synagogue, one of the first Conservative Jewish congregations in the United States. His grandfather was a President of the synagogue and a major donor to it in his day.

When I say it was a central part of our Jewish lives... I know that it shaped who we would become as Jews in ways that we might not have imagined when we joined there.

I was a regular on Shabbat morning... as were my children, my parents and my mother-in-law. We all found our own ways to be active and involved in the ongoing life of this synagogue.

In the second year that we were members at the synagogue a new "young" rabbi came to replace Rabbi Yaacov Rosenberg... a most beloved rabbi to all who were a part of the community. This new "young" rabbi... Rabbi Seymour Rosenbloom would take on a very important role in all of our lives... really becoming a pastor and advisor to the family at many important moments of the life cycle... both difficult and joyous.

Ultimately, for me... Rabbi Rosenbloom would be one of the first to suggest that I too think of becoming a rabbi... and one of my most important advisors in this project. He became not only my rabbi and pastor but a colleague and a friend. He was also very close with my parents and my mother-in-law and sat at their bedside during illnesses... and celebrated with them when that too, was appropriate.

I tell all of this as backdrop.to show just how deep the silence was about my brother after his death.

It is now 1997, twenty five years after Martin's death,. .We have been sitting at my father's bedside for days after he has decided that he wished to go on hospice care after years of struggling with congestive heart disease. In the last hours of his life, Rabbi Rosenbloom has spent hours with him, and my father has shared with the rabbi just how important he has been to him. They prayed together and cried real tears... realizing that this was the end of their time together. It was touching to me to see my colleague so moved by the role that my father had played in his life as a rabbi, in some way we had shared a deep almost "family-like" connection. Rabbi Rosenbloom showed me the importance a rabbi can have in the lives of his congregants.

This type of "pastoring" had become a model to me for how and why I had decided to become a rabbi later in life, and I was now in my third year of a six-year program to become a rabbi. Rabbi Rosenbloom had shown me what a rabbi could be for a family... and I hoped to follow in his footsteps.

In the days that followed my father would pass away at peace at age 93with everyone who loved him having a chance to be by his side. I remained with him until he took his last breath.

And now the surprising part of all of this... in spite of all of these deep and interwoven ways in which Rabbi Rosenbloom was connected to us, he had never even heard that I had an older brother... or that my parent's had had a son...

Rabbi was scheduled to come and meet with the family at my mother's apartment to discuss my father's funeral and the eulogy... and I quickly called him and asked if he could meet me before the family meeting... as I had something important to tell him.

I met the rabbi in the parking lot outside of my mother's apartment building and told him that I had had a brother... Martin... and that it was important for me to tell him about Martin before we met... so that he would know how to talk with my mother about him... and also so that he could publicly acknowledge him in my father's eulogy. There would be people present at my father's funeral, recent friends of my parents who did not know about my brother or his death.

The look of shock on Rabbi's face was real... He was so close with all of us and yet something so central had never been spoken of until this day. It was hard for Rabbi to imagine that the family that he had come to know over all of the years was the same one that I now spoke to him about... a son... one that died so tragically... how could we not have told him?

Yet... this pastor... a master pastor... got it and knew exactly how to open this door that had been locked shut for so many years... with my mother. How to let her know that she was safe to acknowledge this loss now with him and that he too... would know what to do with it.

Rabbi Rosenbloom... our trusted rabbi, friend, colleague... almost like a member of our family... would speak of my brother lovingly... at my father's funeral. He would say his name aloud... and speak gently of the difficulty of the relationship and the difficulty of my brother's life... in a way that honored Martin's role in our family... honored that he was my father's only son. In my father's eulogy were words of honor for my brother that had never been spoken until this point.

At that time of loss... he was able to restore something to our family that had been lost... my brother...

In some way, at my father's funeral, I was also now able to shed the tears that I needed to shed for my brother... not here now to share in this loss with the rest of us.

I would say kaddish for my father and hold my brother with me, when I intoned those words.

Even at the end of life, Mother could not talk about it

WHEN MY FATHER was dying, Jo Ann and I had promised him that we would assure that everything was always good for our mother.

We chose the "best" assisted living facility for her when she became physically disabled. We made sure she had 24 hours of extra help daily to allow her to live a life of dignity and comfort always. My sister and I "were on call" for any need psychological, emotional or physical that mother might have had. We visited her every single day. I ate lunch or dinner with her several times a week. We were true always to the promise we had made to my father.

And yet, Jo Ann and I were not capable of keeping unhappiness from my mother. She would enter seasons of sadness and seeming depression that all of our attention could not alleviate. I finally convinced Mother that perhaps the psychiatrist on staff at her assisted living facility might be of help.

I invite you into the first session that she had with that psychiatrist that took place in her room:

"So Mrs. Hess tell me a little about your life."

"I have been blessed in my life," my mother told her. "I have two wonderful daughters, four outstanding grandchildren and four great grandchildren. My husband and I were always in love until the very end of his life, 58 years of a wonderful marriage. I am living in a nice place here and I have friends. My daughters see to it that I have every single thing that I need every day. So you see, everything has been good for me, until I wound up in a wheelchair."

"Mrs. Hess, is there anything else that might be causing you to feel sad or depressed at this point in your life?"

"No, as I just said, my life has been blessed in so many ways."

I was listening to this interchange, and I asked if I could say anything. The doctor told me I could. So I asked my mother if there was anything at all that might have happened in her life that was very difficult, knowing full well that there was. There was the one thing that any parent could not abide, the death of a child. I just wanted to see if mother would break the silence and allow the psychiatrist to help her with this at the end of her life.

"No," mother said to me, "you know that there isn't." She said this with a somewhat conspiratorial look on her face, entreating me not to "bring it up."

I could not sit still. What was the point of trying to help mother if she would not open up to the young doctor about what was the worst part of her life.

I asked again, "Is it alright if I say something more?"

And the doctor agreed to allow me to.

"You see Doctor, over thirty years ago my brother was murdered in a tragic way. We don't ever talk about this in our family. I have with my children, my husband and my therapist. But as a family we just are forbidden to bring it up. I wonder whether Mother...you might want to explore this with this doctor. Perhaps, at this point in life it might help you to come to some peace with it. I cannot imagine that when you are sitting alone in your room every day that it may not come to you and cause you sadness and depression. This would be a possible time to deal with this."

"No," my mother said. "I have put that away a long time ago and I do not wish to talk about it now, not with you and not with the doctor. It is not the thing that bothers me now. So doctor, if you want to talk with me about my current situation that's fine... but not that!"

And that was the end of that The doctor looked at me with shock and sadness on her own face. Sadness that mother would not really allow her to help, and shock that my mother could not speak of her real sadness and its source.

In the end, she prescribed an anti-depressant for mother... and no talk therapy.

I know that mother was not happy with me for my disclosure. We never discussed it. She just had that look of disapproval on her face for days after that.

I had brought my own values into the equation. I wanted to talk about this part of life. I especially wanted to talk with my mother about it while I still could... and in the presence of another professional. I hoped that this would be possible. But no, it was not even possible then, at the end, while we still had a bit of time.

I wanted mother to "unburden" herself. I wanted her to look at what was making her so sad, when we all worked so hard to make her happier... it was futile.

PART VI

Aftermath

Martin at a more innocent time

Jo Ann

"One of the things you miss when someone dies is the shared fact of 'you Part.' The we of me... in the routine joys; the physical and emotional anchor. We overcome grief merely by outlasting it." —Gail Godwin

I BELIEVE THAT *one of the things we both missed most was the shared fact of "us": the routine joys and sorrows, the physical and emotional anchor of "us." Fredi and I have survived this grief merely by outlasting it.*

When I reflect on this period, I realize the remaining and residual anger I feel currently is the result of all the time silence prevailed. There was no place, other than in therapy, for the release of this anger. It is at the heart of the different way I choose to write from that of my sister... I cannot share her feelings of "the good and innocent" brother she remembers. Too much time has elapsed. Too many events, occasions, troubles, celebrations have transpired... and Martin is not present. That angers me as much as it provokes sorrow. It does not make me want to remember him lovingly... it just makes me angry.

Our children's childhoods as you watch them unscroll are always indexed to our own, visibly and invisibly, their incidents and episodes, pleasures and calamities snarled with our own. My childhood, or my memory of it, is present in every moment of theirs, answering it, prefiguring it, shadowing it. When they arrive they change our present, enlighten or past and brighten our future.

My relationship with my father was different from my siblings. I was the child he favored and probably embraced more frequently. I don't know whether that was because I was female; or because I tried much harder to succeed academically and bring home good news reports. My connection to Daddy remains a pervasive memory as I think about him.

I believe my children were able to coax maternal support and, because of their attachment to their grandparents, our relationship was eventually mended. I was particularly aware of this upon the birth of my first grandchild, Noah. Although dad had died only 6 months prior to his birth, mother wanted to be an integral caregiver when Marci returned from the hospital. She stayed with me in Greenwich for several days demonstrating "the way" to handle a newborn. This was reminiscent of her commitment to me when Rick and Paul were infants. Of course, that preceded Martin's death but she was ever present teaching me in the same manner as when she reached out to Rick and Marci as new parents.

Parenting gave her pleasure. Children gave her pleasure. The business and all of its challenges gave her aggravation. I am not certain, in retrospect, that our father derived the same sense of pleasure from parenting. However, upon Martin's death, he was the only parent that I felt needed and wanted to embrace me... and to ease my pain

There are definitely times when I am reminded of Martin-like characteristics when my grandson, Dovid, tries to "pull a fast one" or charm his way into a situation. I think those attributes were actually derived from our father... something he would never admit because he thought it was a poor reflection of his own behavior. But I believe some of it is in the genes; Martin had it... it didn't come from nowhere... he learned it by observing his father and modeling some of his not-so-pleasing attributes in his own fashion. I wonder what Mother would have to say about that because she never wanted to analyze or to reflect on his behaviors and what made him tick. She just loved each of us for who we were and that was who she was.

What happened to his dog or to his other possessions was never information that was shared with the family. There were a few articles like a ring, a money clip, a liter that I found in drawers when I packed my house to move. How they got there or when I received them I have no recollection. They had no sentimental value for me because his remaining effects made me numb.

Looking through old pictures... trying to discover who you were... who you became; I am struck by how much you are missing. I keep looking for you interacting in my life and in my children's lives. You are not there!! Your absence, in retrospect, has a profound impact on me. What have you missed? What would you have loved? Who would have loved knowing you?

We have not only lost... we have been robbed of your presence... your humor... your insight... your caring... YOU!! This is a painful, yet bittersweet activity... it knows no boundaries. It forces me to consider how you would react to our memoir writing. I believe you would underestimate our ability to know and to convey who you were. Understandably so much of who you became was unknown to us. That was certainly by design and intentional.

The manner by which you chose to achieve, through criminal activities, was foreign and disturbing to me and my family. I didn't want to know what trouble you had gotten yourself into... I was living my life and did not believe your nefarious endeavors would have any impact on me or my family. Of course I was wrong... I was naïve. What did I know about the drug trade or the mafia? Realistically, I didn't want to know.

But reality bites... and in the end, everyone was bitten. With you at the center, so many lives were affected and so many necessary supports were absent and the aftershocks last forever.

Traumatic growth was what led both of us to achieve in many ways: to find personal strengths and to gain appreciation from deep relationships and new possibilities. The need for us to provide a protective cover and close relations with our kids orchestrated our lives.

Fredi: Life went on

IN THE END, the summer of Martin's death the family record notes:

The business... 6914 Torresdale Ave. no longer existed. It had gone into bankruptcy as it had expanded beyond the families capability to maintain it. Also, money had been squandered on my fancy wedding...which I implored them not to do and money was also necessary to bail Martin out and pay legal fees for his lawyers.

Martin had many businesses up in the air all at once... he who did not want to work hard to make money... they were:

- A booth at Jerry's Corner in South Philadelphia selling carpets.
- A drapery business with Paul and Candy Rubin(folks I never heard of until reading about it in the Newspaper 45 years later) in New Jersey.
- Drug smuggling, counterfeiting money, threatening to kill people connected to him and connected to the mob.

My mother returned to nursing after thirty years. She worked as a delivery room nurse and reclaimed who she really was. She was able to utilize her interpersonal talents and her intelligence in this work and feel worthwhile in ways that she never was able to do in the family business with all of its troubles.

My father continued to work out on the street selling wholesale linens, the work he had always enjoyed doing the most. He had to adjust to my mother working the night shift as a nurse which meant that they only slept together on the nights that she was not working. The major source of family income was my mother's job which came with benefits that she had not had working in the business.

All of those quiet and at times not so quiet messages about striving to be successful in life had brought all of us to this very moment. Striving was much more complex than we could ever have imagined.

The legacy of silence

WHEN MY DAUGHTERS were little they were told that my older brother was killed in an automobile accident...which technically was accurate. I believed that as little girls this was what they could understand and that they could say in front of my parents. I was content to leave this as it was until I felt they were old enough to understand.

One Sunday at dinner with my parents and my sister and her children... some topic came up that was related to illegal drugs and the prevalence of drugs in our society. The topic almost... and I emphasize almost...verged into the "forbidden topic"... and as I sat there with my daughters I told myself..." When we get home tonight, I am going to tell them the truth about Martin."

And so, I did. Julie was probably nine years old and Emily, seven. They were both... and are still both brilliant and accomplished abstract thinkers. This allowed me to unfold the story to two young girls and know that they would understand what it meant that Martin had gotten involved with criminals and had become a criminal himself. I knew that I could explain to them about the trial and that he was to testify there against the other criminals. They understood that "telling on the others" was trouble and that was why they had to kill him. They could parrot back to me what they took from hearing this family secret. I also had to explain to them that we "couldn't" talk about this. They asked the reason for the silence and I shared with them that their grandparents could not...would not... ever... talk about this part of their lives and that they did not want any of us to either. They sat quietly and took this information in and then they too began the family routine of quiet on this topic.

I believe that I must have told them if they had any questions that they could come to me and ask me, that was/is generally who I am as a mother. And we talked incessantly about many issues in life... and analyzed the psychological impact of their behavior and the behavior of others... nightly over dinner. Yet my daughters were true to the family contract... this topic was off limits... no questions came and I did not elicit them. I had delivered information... and it was up to them to process on their own, it seems.

My daughters tell me, that even though we did not talk openly again about Martin and his problems they traveled with all of us everywhere.

Their mother who tried to be "perfect" in everything that she did as a mother, a daughter, a friend, a spouse... a professional... taught them daily that in this household, "we must not make mistakes or take chances." Ushered into motherhood as I was, I worked doggedly to try to create a world for my daughters in which life could not go astray for them, as it had for my brother.

I tried to always appear relaxed and easy going but my actions translated mightily that "all of us in the Cooper household can be the best." "Be the best" went everywhere my girls traveled. They were the most gifted students in school and Hebrew school. They were "good campers" at summer camp. They were raised to be moral and ethical in their approach to the world and to others. They were the ones who were expected to be kind and caring to everyone and never !!! be the one to hurt another.

As a result, sometimes they were the ones to be hurt by someone else. They were the ones to play by the rules when someone else might take a chance and break the rules. My younger daughter reported that she never really learned how to cut a corner in life in any area as it was expected that we could and would excel... and we all did.

Yes, it was always there... every day, even and especially in the deep silence.

It took me beginning this project for one daughter to admit to me that as a teenager she had tried to do all of the research I am doing now. Julie, the one born just six days before Martin's death combed the microfiche at the Philadelphia Main Library, when she was in high school, for the newspaper information about Martin's death and the murder trials after his death. She told her father she was doing it and they both kept it to themselves. They believed that it was too difficult for me to know what she had found out. When I ask her about this today she tells me that she kept a folder of the material. She thought that perhaps one day she would write a novel about what she had found. The materials stayed put in the folder she developed. The novel, never to come to fruition. Perhaps, Julie knew that it was not for her to tell this story.

It was for her mother, and her aunt.

We were silent…yet it was always there, even in the next generation.

"Your job for the duration of our lives: You must not hurt us like he did!"

A TALL ORDER indeed...but I took it to heart every day of their lives and worked to assure that I upheld my part of this bargain.

Let's get this straight, they (my parents) never actually said these words but it was understood. And mostly, I was eminently successful in assuring that I only brought good news to my parents to guard them from any additional pain in their lives. My daughters were an easy source of joy for all in the family. They were/are... beautiful, brilliant and kind. My parents got to bask in both of them and all of the things that they had to offer the world... and the family. My husband was successful and always helpful to them. We lived a life that they could only have dreamed of for us...we had a beautiful home, private schools for the girls, summer camp, vacations, and two cars parked in the driveway. This was what they had hoped for.

And their daughter... I was no slouch either. I had gotten a doctoral degree and ran a school and then had a thriving private practice. So every day...was a good one filled with the reports that helped to keep them in a state of ease.

That is until I got sick.

At age 42 I developed an illness that was difficult to diagnose. I ran fevers for over a year, and had ongoing digestive issues. I continued to lose weight without trying... something that was totally aberrant in a person who had always been chubby and had difficulty not gaining weight. I had the best doctors in the Philadelphia area stumped about what was wrong with me and we all just watched as I became a shadow of myself.

Remember, I was not to cause them pain… like he had. It seemed like we might all be on course for me to shatter that rule.

My parents were suffering now because of me and I was aware of this daily. I tried whatever I could to lessen their fear and sadness, but after all I was the patient, and I was not playing this role with my full emotional or physical strength, as I was just trying to survive.

When it was determined that I needed major surgery to both diagnose and treat this mystery ailment we all tried to "put on a good face" before the surgery. It would be even a more difficult recovery as I was in a deteriorated state of health going into the surgery.

More than anything else pre-surgery… I worried about my parents. I somehow knew that I had less to worry about with my daughters, my husband, my sister… or myself. It was them… it was always them… I could not bear the look on their faces when they saw me… and they saw how sick I was. I was hurting them… I could not protect them.

When I awakened from the surgery in the recovery room I realized that I was hooked up to so many lines, bags, machines… and my first thought was: "With all of this stuff, how will I be able to fool my parents into thinking that I am really OK?" My own pain… or the implications of all of the machines for me… were quite secondary.

I vowed to myself… when I am taken back to my post-operative room… if they are sitting there I will show them that in spite of all of the contraptions I feel "fine!"

If my mouth was free of encumberance… it would voice the emotions and the truths that my mother and father needed… I would tell them, enact for them… the physical strength that I had to recover from this terrible illness… I would immediately embody resilience… I would try to put their minds at ease.

I would be sure to let them know… "I will not die"… trust me… I won't do what he did…

And I am sorry, so sorry that I have caused both of you to have that look of despair on your faces… due to me. I will make it up to you… in any way that I am able.

So as I was wheeled into my room… I was babbling on to all who were present about how great I felt and how much easier the entire surgery had actually been. I made jokes about all of the tubes and lines emerging from me… and I entreated my sister to "wash my hair" as soon as possible so that I would look the best I could.

Yes… see I am fine! Mom and Dad… just fine… and I will get better… I will use every fiber of my being to do so… in order that I can be "your best daughter again." One who will not cause you pain… not now… not ever.

I have no idea if they were able to take in the burden that they had placed on my shoulders. They did not seem to see that my daughters and my husband were as scared as they were. They did not seem to see that I was terrified… how could they when I worked mightily to "fool them."

Martin caused them pain and fought them every inch of the way.

I caused them pain… and I held them… and hid my own pain… to make sure they remained safe in their lives.

"Never hurt us, like he did!"

How is this possible, Martin says

FLASH FORWARD. IT is Yom Kippur of 2000... another large and impressive Conservative synagogue just up the road by several miles from where this scene had happened perhaps 40 years before. There is marble and gold and thousands of congregants... as at Emanu-el... there is pomp and ceremony here too. But now... there are two rabbis on the bimah... one Rabbi Seymour Rosenbloom... and one Rabbi Fredi Hess Cooper... that's right... the little sister from above.

My brother... dead now on this Yom Kippur scene for over 28 years... not present to see that his sister had held tightly to the tradition that I had shared with him. So much of who he was had shaped this new rabbi... both the fun and the issues that made her furious with him.

This would be my first High Holiday season as a rabbi... my first time not sitting in the seats in the imposing service. The first time that I would be responsible for the inspiration of others, on this day. Somehow... I brought him with me...... I imagined him again sneaking into this synagogue(which also required the ticket to get in)... and looking up on the bimah and finding his "little sister" in the rabbinic robe and at the podium speaking to the congregation. I imagined the shock on his face to find me here... and I knew that only he knew how he had tried his hardest... to lead me away from the seriousness of the day of Yom Kippur. Had he been there to actually witness this... he may have tried with me again to reduce me to laughter when I was to be solemn! I knew in my heart that he in fact had led me exactly to this moment. I wished that in this fantasy... I could reach him... or I could reach someone sitting there that day like him... to find the way in... the way back to this rich tradition. The synagogue… the place that he and my family spent so many hours in… had led him in… and led him away. As in many of the roads that I had traveled to this point… I hoped that I could touch someone… in the way I wished someone had touched my brother. It was my belief that within this house of worship there was the way to right the course of one's life… just as we pray for on Yom Kippur.

Where the hell are you when I need you!

THE END... MOTHER IS dying... another hospice watch... it is my job to sit here until the end...

Mother made it clear to me over and over again that "she was not to die all alone" she wanted someone with her until her last breath. She had watched me sit with my father at the end of his life... even when she could no longer sit there.

She had learned... as my father too learned... that I was the one in the family that could do this last job for those I loved. I would be there as long as the process would take. I would not abandon my beloved parents when they needed a companion to reach the end of life.

We all learned that together when daddy was dying. It was not a natural job for my sister. She was too close to daddy and too angry that he had decided he was too tired to go on. This chapter was too hard for her... and though she acted as though she was angry with me for sitting there with him... she really was angry that she would lose her dad... her closest family connection. So she let me be the one... the one to grasp his hand, the one to sing prayers to him... the one to make Havdalah a ceremony marking separations in his room, when Shabbat exited and he was still alive. Even though he was in and out of consciousness... he still got it... it was about Shabbat leaving yet one more time... but it was about his leaving the world of the living as well. He opened his eyes to let me know that he got it. Within the next day while I held his hand, he took his last breath. It was for me to call and tell my sister and my mother that the end had come.

So mother and my sister knew that when it was time for mother to be at the end, it would be me again that would sit and hold on until the last breath. And mother issued that instruction repeatedly to assure that she knew that I understood that she meant it…"I don't want to be alone when I die… nothing could be worse than that."

And so there I was again in the hospice room, watching mother's every breath.

It was supposedly "dark and soothing" in the room… the shades drawn and few sounds besides her uneven breaths. But both Jo Ann and I were bothered daily with a harpist that came and played maudlin songs outside of Mother's room… never invited in as Mother would have hated the music as much as Jo Ann and I hated it!

While we were quite sure that mother would not appreciate the harpist she did react to music. She liked my singing… often tunes that she liked and sometimes even for my non-believing mother a prayer or two. While I chanted and she heard my voice, she seemed to be at peace.

And for mother, I would not get up at all. I was too afraid that if I left the room she would feel abandoned. I constantly let her know I was there.

These were the moments when I asked Martin…" Where the hell are you when I need you the most!"

I knew were he alive he would have been at my side in mother's last days. She was the one he had been most connected to… she was the one that loved him unconditionally and he her. Theirs was a bond that was unequalled in the family. Mother could always find the sweet side of him..

As I sat with her and longed for his presence at her death bed it became clear yet one more time just how devastating it had been for her to lose him there were no words that she could say to any of us that would capture the sense of utter terror and horror she experienced in his loss. He was her heart; he was the one who needed her love the most. He was hers.

She could not tell any of us this. She had to soldier on, the stoic, and just live life without him… and she did.

There were no words…

So there I was without him to help me. I knew that he too would have taken her hand and assured her that we would not leave… until she did.

Of course there were others who came and went each day. My children, my sister's children, my husband... and my sister... they were all there to let mother know we loved her and would hold each other close in her absence.

But each of them came and went... Only I stayed planted by her side.

"Mother, I am just going to step into the bathroom for two minutes... don't go anywhere while I am in there!"

This routine would repeat each day... literally as needed.

Finally, on that last morning I just had to take a shower. I could not wait another day. I told mother that I needed to do so and I implored her to realize this time it would be ten minutes... but I would be back as soon as possible.

I was good to my word. I showered in record time... with a little piece of a towel to dry off with and threw my clothes back on in haste.

"Mother, I am back and cleaner and I will not leave your side now at all... you are free to be with me until you cannot anymore."

And so, she and I sat... she barely taking a breath any more... me cleaner but steadfast at her side. I knew now that it would be just hours until the last breath would come... I was there... as promised.

I think I felt him with me at her side. I think I saw him on the other side of that bed grasping her other hand tightly. He was whispering to her that she could now come his way... come back to him so many years later.

Ok... so you came, Martin, and sat with me after all when I most needed you, and when mother needed you, just like we did together so many years ago. Each of us, holding one hand. I will let go of mother's hand now knowing that you are taking her with you now. Thank you for helping me to let her go.

And now they are gone... first Martin, then Daddy and now Mother...

She was the one that I thought I could never release... but her hand is cold now... and I knew I could let go. I had done what she had asked, really every single day since you left us Martin. So I could let go knowing that that part of my life was, in fact, now complete.

And now I could turn my face out again to my own family... and to my sister...

My sister, she and I would/will always walk together to remember and cherish the family we all were.

And through it all... there was always love...

February 2018

IT'S AN UNUSUALLY sunny spring-like February morning. I am sitting in the sun-filled library having my morning cup of ginger- infused tea and reading the morning papers. This is a very sacred part of my day and in my retirement, I relish the fact that I can take my time with it. I always read the Philadelphia Inquirer first. The first page of the paper has a headline about a well-known mob figure and a trial that was to begin that day. I am drawn to anything written about organized crime families. In the first paragraph a name catches my eye...

"Mr. Merlino, is accompanied to the courthouse by his lawyer, Joseph Santaguida well-known for his defense of figures in the world of organized crime."

Oh my...Joseph Santaguida... my brother's lawyer.

Forty five years later... finally... someone is still alive! That was my first reaction. I sat there with iPhone in hand immediately googling...Joseph Santaguida. I located him! Martin's lawyer was alive and still in practice and was in my city... I could talk with someone who really knew this part of my brother!

And so I wrote the number on a piece of paper... consulted with no one about it first... grabbed for the phone dialed the first two numbers and stopped... dead in my tracks...

I felt a panic come over me... the fear that I felt froze my fingers and would not allow me to dial the remainder of the number...

In my head I heard the voice saying... this is ridiculous the way you are acting...you can finally talk to a real live person about your brother who knew him and knew those final months of his life...you can finally ask someone some of the questions that you have harbored for so many years. Mr. Santaguida why did my brother take the rap for that entire drug deal? Mr. Santaguida, how come my brother was so poorly protected by the government? Mr. Santaguida, why didn't you encourage my brother to trust his family more and use us as character witnesses? The questions I could think to ask were endless, and yet, fear stopped me dead in my tracks.

I could not continue. I put the phone down and felt a bit sick inside. My rational side...was saying to me..."you don't know anything at all about this lawyer and why he has spent over fifty years working as an attorney for mob related criminals... and then all of the "what ifs" came flooding into my being... the ones that we as a family had buried so many years ago to assure we would all be safe. What if he told someone that I contacted him? What if he knew that I should not be opening this case again and that I could get hurt? What if one of the men was still alive and Mr. Santaguida let that "old man" know that the Hess family had resurfaced 45 years later wanting to avenge Martin's murder. What if somehow someone could hurt one of the people I loved most? What if...

And so... I just could not complete that call. And that call gave me a peak into the terror my brother felt for his family, and then my own parents felt after his death. Silence was the better path to stay on.

Reading my relationship with my brother through the lens of Torah

MY FAVORITE AMERICAN holiday is Thanksgiving. It is the one national holiday that as Jews, we can join wholeheartedly in celebration with everyone else . And we have much to be thankful for, we live well in this land filled with abundance. It is generally right around Thanksgiving that we read this parashah, the weekly Torah reading that deals with the reunion of Jacob and Esau in Genesis. It is entitled, Vayislach. I am always struck with the reunion of Jacob and Esau and its poignancy. I have spoken about siblings forced to sit at the table together on this holiday and not always in a loving manner.

So I imagine my brother and I...

We were not twins, my brother and I, he being the oldest and I being the youngest. Yet it seemed in many ways that he and I resembled Jacob and Esau.

My brother was like Esau. He was cunning and clever, always spinning some scheme, always hunting for some angle to win without doing all of the work. He looked rough and brash, even as a child. He was in constant pursuit of smashing the middle class mold of the nice Jewish boy. He was my mother's favorite, her confidante and her support. She claimed to love him in a special way because he was different and often in trouble. She said he needed her love more than I did or than my sister. Her love she believed, was a way of possibly steering him away from his troubling ways..." his hunting out in the field (like Esau) for game. My brother's wild game was often a shady business deal. His final hunt for game leading him to illegally import "hashish" into the country over 45 years ago.

Like Jacob, my life concerns were with finding love in my life and in starting a family. Martin, the Esau character, went off to his own land, one that was totally foreign to our family.

While I, and my sister, could receive the blessing from our parents for all of the ways we pleased them... no blessing would ever come to my brother.

He could wail and scream, and at times he did, but because his ways were foreign to us, we were all hurt by him and there was no way to make amends. His behavior cancelled any chance that he could receive a blessing from my father. Unlike the biblical story, it was Martin who was sent away, it was he who had to live in fear for his life... in the foreign land that he now inhabited.

So many years... a reunion at the Thanksgiving table, not possible. I have been journeying all of these years to find a substitution for this reunion. When I picture him still in my life, I believe that his face has been for me, like seeing the face of God. The face of God that has shaped me over and over in my life.

Thoughts of him will always smolder in me... Esau (Martin) my brother.

How I wish I could run to him now, after all of these words and embrace him and share with him my greater understanding of who he was. I would tell Martin now, that I told his story just as he had wished it to be told.

I would let him know that he had caused me to struggle with the divine, and the struggle has come to clarify who I am in life. In this struggle I have only now found a way to live "shalem" whole...complete... without him. It is my hope that my words now are a blessing for Martin the one he lacked in his life.

Forgiveness

I SIT IN my seat for the service in which we remember and mourn those we have lost in our family... and amongst our people. I am a participant this morning in this part of the service, another rabbi is leading. This will allow me to actually do my own personal reflection and remembering.

Rabbi Debrah asks us to sit back and close our eyes and relax while she guides us through an introspective meditation.

"Picture the person who is no longer with you and that you mourn who you need to forgive" (this being the season of asking forgiveness). Act as though that person is standing before you... think about what you want to say to them to convince them that they are forgiven for acts that impacted you in your life and in your relationship to that person."

I follow her instructions and I picture Martin.

Later she instructs:

"Picture a person who is no longer with you and that you mourn who you need to ask forgiveness from. Act as though that person is standing before you... think about what you want to say to them to convince them that you sincerely seek their forgiveness for acts you perpetrated against them in their life and in your relationship with that person."

I follow her instructions and I picture Martin.

It is not a surprise that this was my meditation. I have now been with Martin almost daily for over a year. I have studied him. I have studied us, his family. I have studied our culture. I have studied the case the government brought against him. I have studied the people he had gotten involved with.

I have written, and read and researched. In all of this I have already followed the first instruction.

I have been eager to offer forgiveness to Martin and this forgiveness flowed with ease. I have wept for him; I have missed him in ways that I had forgotten. I have come to understand him so much better. I have thrown off the extreme anger that I felt, that we all felt… in the last six months of his life… and then in his death. My forgiveness comes from a place that acknowledges all of the pain that he had caused our family, and especially my parents, and yet he was the one who had lost his life… and ended his life so alone.

We all remained standing, never quite the same, but still intact.

But asking Martin to forgive me, that I never did. In this process I realize that there are so many ways that we all failed him, and I personally failed him.

Forgive me Martin because:

I only knew one part of you and was so satisfied with that

I asked for you to "provide" things for my life and I doubt that I reciprocated.

When I knew you were in trouble, I never asked you anything about it… I abandoned you.

I hated the "new" Martin that I only knew for several months, and I held onto that hatred of you. I let the words I hate you pour from my mouth to my husband so many years ago.

I was limited and naïve about the world and life and that eliminated the opportunity for any real connection to you.

I thought I was better than you.

I never adequately thanked you for all of the positive parts of our relationship.

I was proud of you when it was good for me and I was ashamed of you when it was not good for me.

So many things I needed to ask your forgiveness for, I am sure I have not thought of them all. But it helped me on Yom Kippur to believe that I could still ask for this now, so many years later.

My rational self, understood that morning that in picturing you I was really asking myself for forgiveness for all of the ways I shortchanged our relationship so many years ago. I want to believe that had I really asked you, we had enough between us that we would have found a way to make the forgiveness work for both of us. I think you would have forgiven me, and thus your memory has helped me to offer myself similar forgiveness.

Having you with me in my consciousness this past year, has helped in so many ways. Most significant was hearing your voice tell an author that you wanted your story told, if anything happened to you.

It has taken me(us) too long to actually get down to doing this... but now we are. This effort too, is my way of asking for your forgiveness.

Redemption is always possible.

Sheyheyanu: Blessed art thou, God of the Universe that you have brought us alive to see this day.

THIS IS WHERE it all ends for me. I have reached a day where the open wound of loss of my brother has been healed.

I could say I don't know what has finally brought me here... but that would be a lie. I came to this moment by finally looking fully at his life and my life... and my family's life. Many times in the months of writing and reading there was the urge to stop this process... to let it go and re-capture the peace that has prevailed over the years without him in my life. But he was never actually missing. He was with me, shaping every aspect of who I have become as a woman, both my flaws and my strengths.

I end with understanding that we were a good family... better than many... who lacked the resources and sophistication to fully help my brother when it was needed to do so. We never abandoned loving one another, even in the darkest seasons. The memories of love we shared has always inspired me to love.

This moment, this time of redemption, is one for both my image of my brother and my understanding of my family. So many moments over these years I thought that we were all a failed bunch who had let something so evil happen to Martin. Our greatest failing was lack of knowledge and broken communication when it was most needed. We may have seen what was wrong, but we often overlooked it and often did not speak together as a family... of what it was and what we could do together to help. So many years ago we did not know enough about how to help. There were painful memories to re-visit. These have impelled me in life to mitigate the pain of others.

In my travels, I have still seen and known Martin, and all of us.

I have seen his face often... and in those soft and warm eyes I have rekindled all of the tender parts of our relationship. I have seen those short stubby fingers of his... fashioning something beautiful out of nothing at all. His hands I have come to realize were the same hands of my father. Strong hands for both of these men I loved.

I have been brought to this moment, and for this I am forever grateful. There is peace in knowing that in the late season of life I have been able to learn again what was precious. I have been brought here to realize that you were and still are a rich part of my life, and that our imperfect family was still a family filled with warmth and love.

Epilogue

Jo Ann

"How can the dead be truly dead when they still live in the souls of those who are left behind?" —Carson McCullers, The Heart is a Lonely Hunter

IN THE END, *I am troubled by how much of my brother's devastation belongs to me. How can I evaluate this accurately in retrospect?! Is there a score to be settled in this tale that I have told? What remains that is endearing? Enduring? I cannot turn to the torah or tanach for salvation. I am not so aligned with Judaic beliefs that I can find consolation in their script.*

Dani Shapiro relates: "one of the greatest gifts of writing a memoir is having a way to shape chaos: looking at all the pieces side by side so that they make more sense." At the gut level, this is what I struggle with most: matching Fredi's memories with mine.

One may begin writing by freezing a moment in time but I have found that the pain of the moment engraves a deeper, more troubling memory. My sister's need to research, corroborate, substantiate and authenticate bears witness to the event and to all corresponding activities that led up to it. But, for me, the process is one that reminds lots of pain in untold ways. Often searching for clarity results in confusion.

So I return to the explosion. 47 years later it reverberates in my soul. I find I cannot extricate myself from this feeling: there's little comfort or catharsis only the more troubling conceit of why??

- *did we do nothing to prevent it?*
- *did we not speak about it to anyone?*
- *did we not derive calmness from the work of writing the memoir?*
- *did we never share our feelings?*
- *did we not support each other?*

In writing memoir, we live the epilogue of our lives. This may be the hardest part of the whole process because we, as writers, have little control upon what readers, especially family members, will focus. There will be ripple effects of emotions and questions and concerns about what's been included and what's been omitted... and why. Memoir is not about us, what we did or did not do... it's about what we did with what happened to us.

I have compared our work together to a parallelogram: a four sided flat shape with straight sides: where opposite sides are both parallel and equal. If the parallelogram is split in the middle, the result is two triangles; each triangle representing each of our perspectives. This construct has been useful for me as I could envision one of those triangles as a "wedge" between us rather than as the cement that has welded us together.

If one thinks of memoir as a prism: there is shining light or pure or direct light on the past. Therefore, my side reflects what's true for me... my sister's is another angle.

It is my hope that our story melds together in distinctive ways: featuring our separate voices and singular connection. This effort has brought us closer together and has united our memories. In the end, I am left with the questions: did we grow as a result of this writing? And do I still harbor anger about a past I cannot change?

At this juncture, I am struck by contemplating what you, Martin, would make of this feckless attempt to memorialize your life. I am certain you would find it comical... a waste of time... why bother? It was a life that came to no good end. However, over time, I have come to believe it is a story worth telling.

August 7, 2019

Dear Martin,

Today is the 47th anniversary of the day you were murdered. I wanted to give you a follow-up to the invitation that you issued for your two sisters to write the story that you wanted told in that last year of your life. I began this project two years ago and quickly I invited Jo Ann to join me on this journey. It has allowed both of us to finally come to terms with what your death meant to each of us and to our family. Martin, in this long project I have recaptured you and my relationship to you. I have come to know the parts of you that I did not know at the end of your life. I have relished retrieving all of the precious memories of my childhood and young adulthood spent with you.

Right now, I will speak to you only for myself. From the day that you died I harbored an outsized feeling of anger toward you for how your folly had impacted our family. I believe I was mostly angered about what you had done to our parents, who I felt did not deserve this horror in their lives. I treasured our parents and our family as a "good, loving" family, and your involvement in crime and your murder left me feeling that this was a bit of a fraud. So the anger that began on that day made me feel justified in pushing your memory out of my life. It allowed me to embrace the family "vow of silence" concerning everything that involved you and your demise. At that time, when I was so young and unknowing, it felt like the better part of wisdom to follow such a course. You became from that moment on our family "secret."

What I really know though was that you were never truly far from my thoughts. As I had become a mother just the week before your murder, everything that I did in the raising of my two daughters was influenced both by what had been good in my time as your sister, and what had been difficult. I know that my parenting allowed both of them to become strong, brilliant, women. However, my parenting was also overlaid by a quiet anxiety that I "would never repeat our parents mistakes," with my own children. It was a burden to fulfill this mantra as a mother and I am aware that what I thought of as "quiet anxiety" was translated mightily to both of them. My daughters have told me that you were actually present in our lives always. Today I recognize that your presence was not always difficult it was also always tinged with the joy for life that you bestowed on me.

I have come to understand so much more about who you, my brother, really were. I want you to know that I do love you, in your entirety. Martin, I think you were always searching for yourself in life and in a family that did not always fit with your conception of who you were. So many years ago, the Hess family was incapable of embracing who you truly were. Your self-definition was not in sync with the time that you lived your life. The most important thing that I learned in my research and writing is that in the end you actually tried to do the right thing. Our parents asked you to be a "mensch" and turns states evidence, and as asked, you did so. At least one judge, in his words concerning you, acknowledged that you had helped the government in so many ways to unravel a terrible group of criminals that were functioning across our country. When I read your testimony in court records I obtained, I "heard" your voice as the brother that I knew. Your answers were articulate and well thought out and reflected a naïve innocence about all you had involved yourself with. You sounded confused but I heard that you worried about your family knowing everything about you, and that you worried about others who you were connected with. In your confusion, I heard a young man that was capable or being responsible and loving of others. And for this help that you provided well, you went unprotected and for this you lost your life. That same judge expressed deep anger that you were allowed to be murdered, as you had become quite valued by the system. This process has had me re-evaluating who you were in the end. It has corrected my view of you at the very end of your life as a "mob criminal" to a victim of two very difficult systems. You were caught between the world of organized crime and the federal government. In offering fealty to our government you wound up being a victim. It is crazy that I lived so many years with a lack of understanding of this very basic fact. I have learned through this to place my anger in the proper place. It was the criminals and the government officials who were the real culprits.

Martin, it saddens me greatly that on that last day of your life, you were so alone. Your family had little ability to really support you and show up by your side when it was most needed. I also learned that the man who you loved the most, Joey, had turned on you in the very end. I regret that the love that you deserved in life, was absent when you needed it most. For this, and so much more, I finally ask your forgiveness.

I want you to know that you continue to be my teacher in life. After all of the pain that you endured in your life, you have helped me to be the best "helper" that I can be to others. You also instructed me in every aspect of my life about "how to have fun," and push against my tendency to be so straight-laced. Whenever I have found a way to do something even a bit crazy, it is your voice coaching me to really try it and to laugh in the process. I know that this has allowed me to be accessible to many young people who I have helped in life both as a therapist and as a rabbi. And that last part, the rabbi, I thank you for making the synagogue somehow magical for me. As you led me through the "secret passageways" of our synagogue you were imprinting something in my soul that remained with me always and pushed me later in life to make this my life's work. Even that little sukkah you built with me has remained so important that you stand at my side coaching me, yearly now, as I erect my own sukkah.

So, my beloved brother, your sisters have done as you wished. We have spent two years crafting your story and within it a bit of our own stories, as well. This process has been one of the most meaningful trips of my life. The best part of it has been that you have been with me again, every day for these two years. I have learned finally, that even in your absence you have always been with me, gently influencing my path in life.

I miss you Martin. I am grateful that you pushed me to re-visit our lives.

With deep love and gratitude,
Fredi

Dear Jo Ann and Fredi,

All that I need to say to both of you now is, thank you. I wanted my story told and you have done it. Now I am at peace.

I too express deep love and gratitude,

Martin

Endnote

Fredi

IN THE FALL of 2017, after just a few months of working on this book, I realized that I needed to see if there were any court proceedings that still existed that might shed further light on all that had transpired. My first foray was to request documents from the Philadelphia Courts where Martin had been tried. I sent off requests to their archives and found that I had contacted them just in time to retrieve some of these records, as the records are not kept forever.

It was the director of the archives in the Federal Court located at 6th and Market streets in Philadelphia who educated me about requesting records about this case from the FBI. I told him why I was doing this research and his response was: "Rabbi this is quite a case involving your brother and his death and how it was handled, but we only possess a fraction of the records that reflect the complexity of the case. You need to file a FOIA request to obtain the remainder of the records. These records will still be accessible if you are willing to pay for their duplication."

I assured him that I would pay almost anything to read the records but I had never even heard of a FOIA request until he had uttered this directive. He wrote down how to find the website and then he encouraged me to follow through on this. Literally, as soon as I returned home I went on the website and immediately followed their directions for filing such a request.

I learned that if your case is: "simple and straightforward you may receive the records within 6 months' time. If the request is more complex it may take one year to a maximum of two years to obtain the records related to the case.

So after a year and still no word, I spoke directly to someone at the FBI records division who explained that just as an agent was about to be in touch with me they were made aware that "Other Government Agencies" were involved in my brother's case and thus each of them would have to review the documents and give their okay for their release and that this would greatly slow down the process.

Clearly, Martin's involvement and his murder were far more complex than we were able to understand.

Finally, in January 2020, I get a "final decision" about the documents that can be shared with me from the Department of Justice. The packet includes four pages explaining why they are sharing what they are sharing and then eight pages of basically redundant and repetitive text about my brother's murder. There are also redactions in these scant pages. But my wait was not entirely in vain, there are a few things I learned:

- My brother's car that my sister and I remembered to be a convertible was a hard- topped vehicle
- His flashy car was registered in my father's name. This is an additional piece of evidence to me that even with this car that screamed "I am a mobster," my parents were needed to actualize his possession of it.
- Martin had been arrested three times on narcotics charges. We were aware of only one arrest in the last months of his life.
- It was stated that besides these three arrests his only other charges were traffic violations.
- In 1972 they stated: "Mr. Hess seemed to display homosexual tendencies." This was truly a sign of the times underscoring that this too was evidence that he was "aberrant" and this might indicate criminal behavior.
- They noted that his death was considered to be an "obstruction of justice."

www.ingramcontent.com/pod-product-compliance
Lightning Source LLC
LaVergne TN
LVHW090319160826
845684LV00011B/71/J

* 9 7 9 8 9 8 7 2 2 1 2 0 4 *